Handwriting Without Tears®
by Learning Without Tears

Name:

Cursive Success

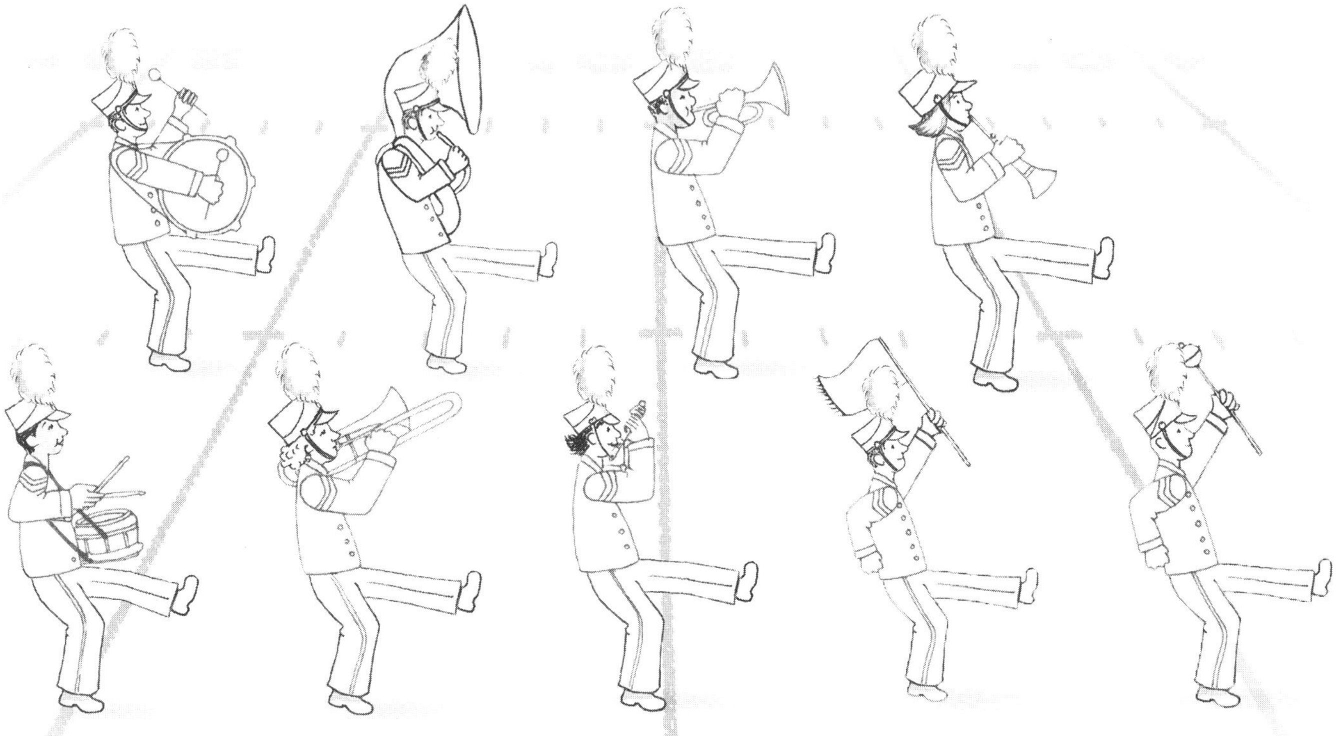

drums   rhythm   march

LEARNING
Without Tears®

8001 MacArthur Blvd
Cabin John, MD 20818
LWTears.com | 888.983.8409

Author: Jan Z. Olsen, OTR
Content Advisors: Christina Bretz, MS, OTR/L, Tania Ferrandino, OTR/L
Illustrators: Jan Z. Olsen, OTR, Julie Koborg, Carol Johnston, Sammie Simon
Graphic Designers: Carol Johnston, Julie Koborg
Editors: Annie Cassidy, Megan Parker

January 2, 2022

Dear Student,

Can you read this? It's cursive. Cursive is connected handwriting. Students like the way it makes their writing look more grown up.

At first, cursive takes more time, but with practice you'll find it faster than print and just as neat. As you master cursive, you will develop your own personal style. I hope you enjoy this book.

Sincerely,
Jan Z. Olsen

Aa Bb Cc Dd Ee Ff Gg Hh Ii Jj Kk Ll Mm
9   36   8   10   15   17   11   12   22   23   26   16   42

TABLE OF CONTENTS

Preparing for Cursive

Lowercase Letters
Magic c Letters

Lowercase: h t p

Lowercase: e l f

Lowercase: u y i j

Lowercase: k r s

Tow Truck Letters: o w b v

Cursive Lowercase

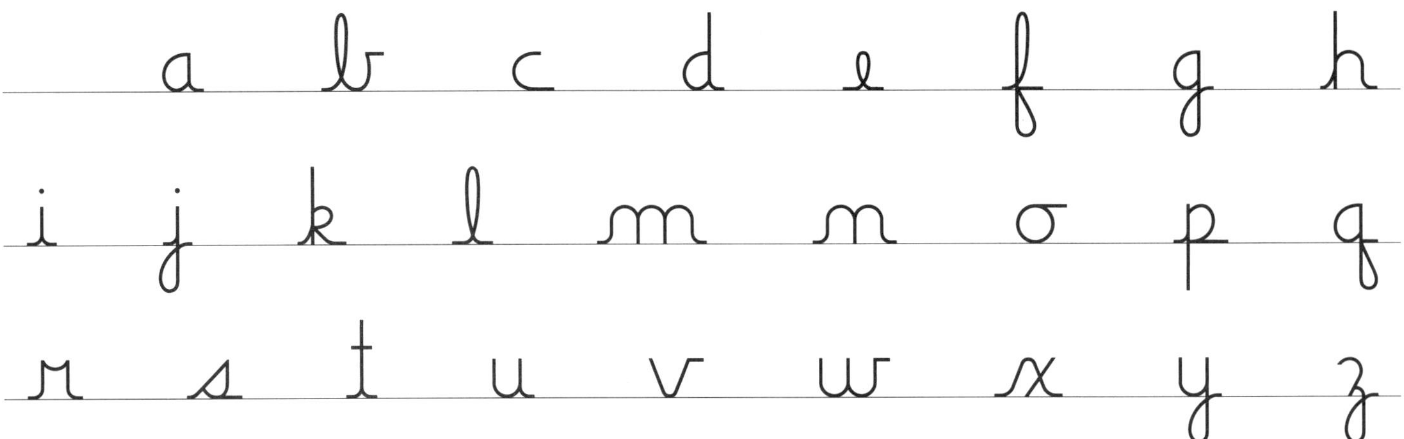

Connection Rule: When two letters are connected, the first letter is the "boss" of the connection.

1. Base line connections: If the first letter ends on the base line (22 letters), start the next letter on the base line.
2. High connections: If the first letter ends high (Tow Truck Letters: o, w, b, v), start the next letter high.

Cursive Capitals

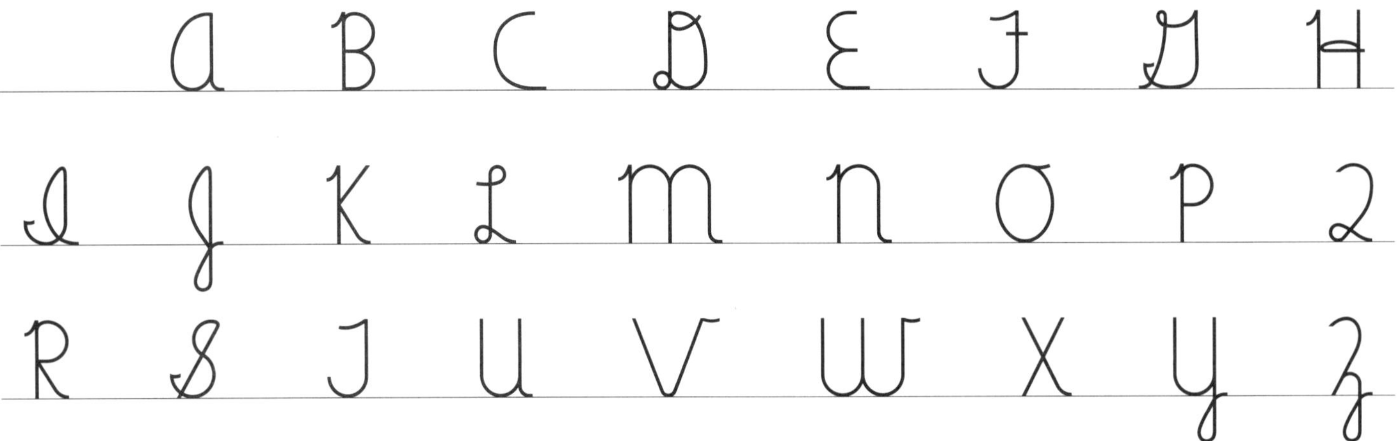

Connection Rule: Capitals do not have to connect.

1. Connect if it's easy; the capital ends on the base line and on the right side.
2. Don't connect if it's tricky, a high ending, or wrong side.

Cursive Warm-Ups

Under and over **Up and straight down** **Up and loop down** **Descending loop**

Start on the star. Do one row a day.

Cursive Name

Write your name on regular double lines. For help, look at the opposite page or ask your teacher.

Name:

Now try your name on narrow double lines.

Name:

Cursive Success

Paper Placement & Pencil Skills

LEFT-HANDED

Place the **left** corner higher.

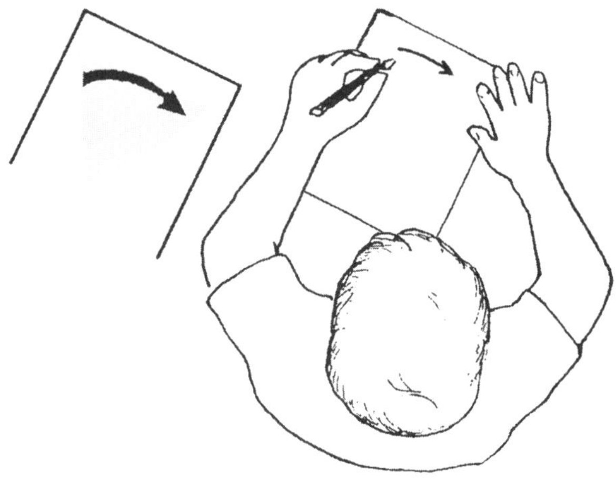

RIGHT-HANDED

Place the **right** corner higher.

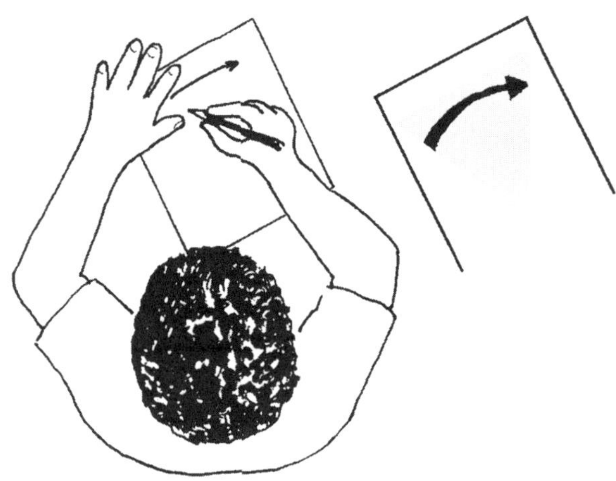

Standard grip: Hold pencil with **thumb + index finger.** Pencil rests on middle finger.

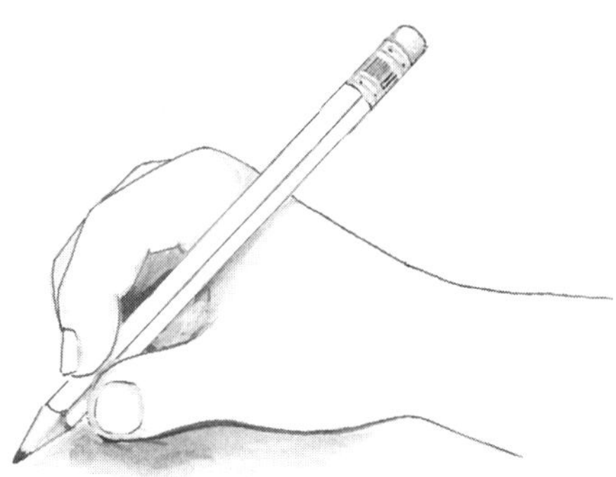

Eraser points to **left** shoulder.

Eraser points to **right** shoulder.

Alternate grip: Hold pencil with **thumb + index and middle fingers.** Pencil rests on ring finger.

Learn & Check

Learn letters, words, sentences, and how to check them.
When you see the box ☐, it's time to check your work.

☑ **Check letter** Teachers: Help children ☑ their letter for correct start, steps, and bump.

1. Start correctly.

2. Do each step.

3. Bump the lines.

☑ **Check word** Teachers: Help children ☑ their word for correct letter size, placement, and connections.

1. Make letters the correct size.
2. Place letters correctly: tall, small, or descending.

3. Connect letters correctly.

Tall   **Small**   **Descending**

☑ **Check sentence** Teachers: Help children ☑ their sentence for correct capitalization, word spacing, and ending punctuation.

1. Start with a capital.

2. Put space between words.

3. End with . ? or !

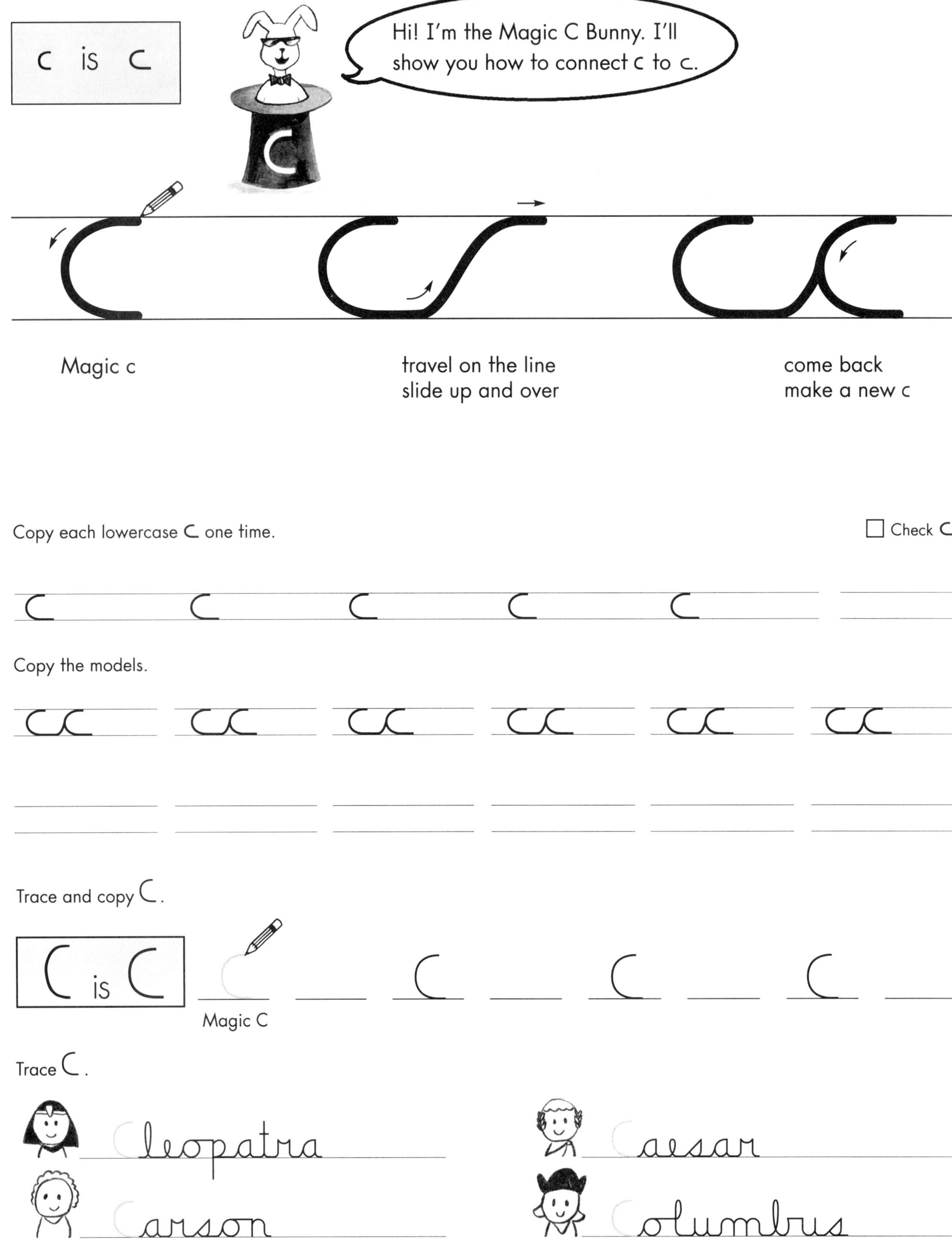

Copy each lowercase C one time.

☐ Check C

Copy the models.

Trace and copy C.

C is C

Magic C

Trace C.

☑ Check letter.   Teachers: Help children ✔ their word for correct start, steps, and bumps.

    © 2022 Learning Without Tears

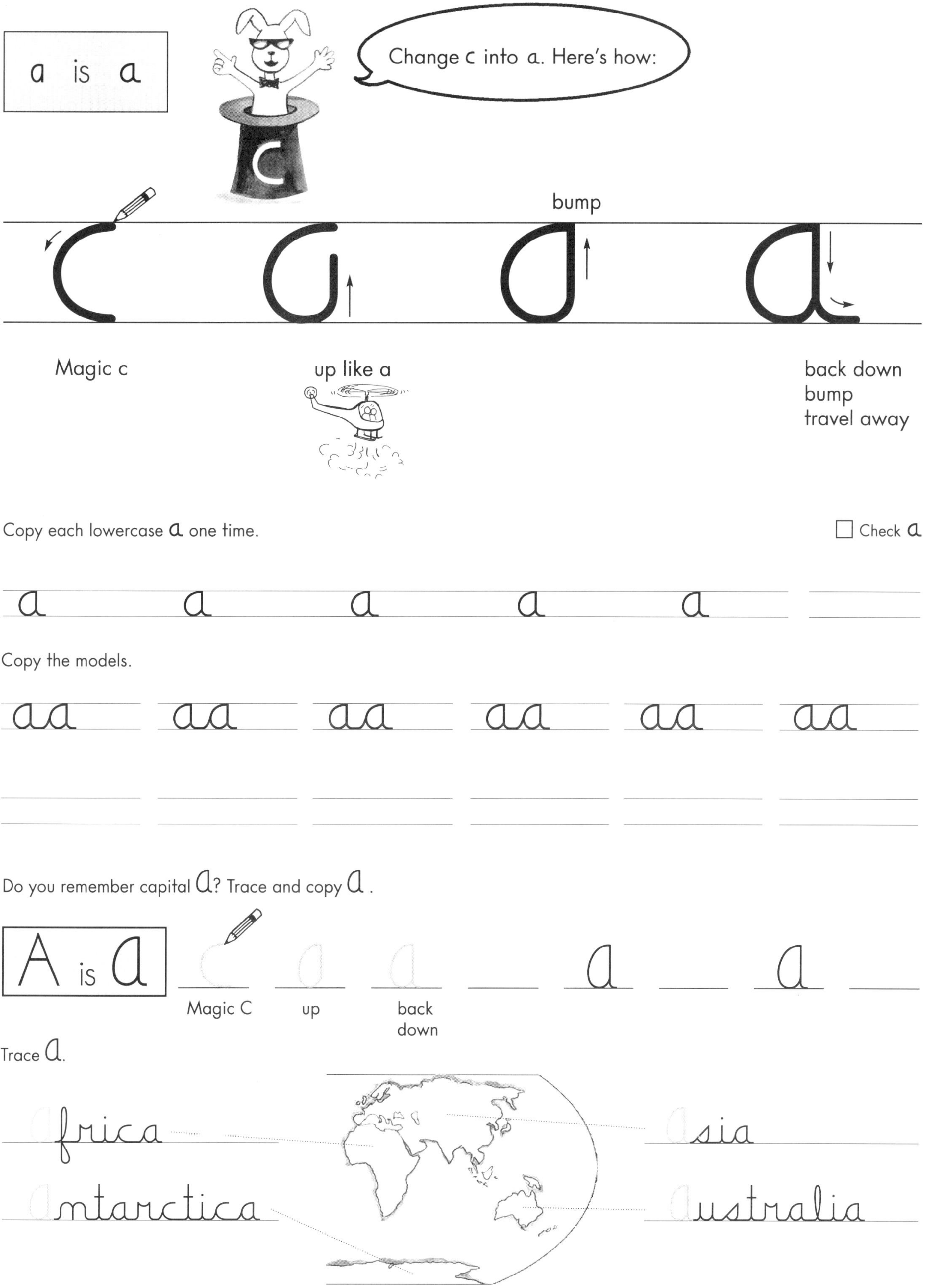

a is a

Copy each lowercase a one time.   ☐ Check a

Copy the models.

Do you remember capital a? Trace and copy a.

A is a

Trace a.

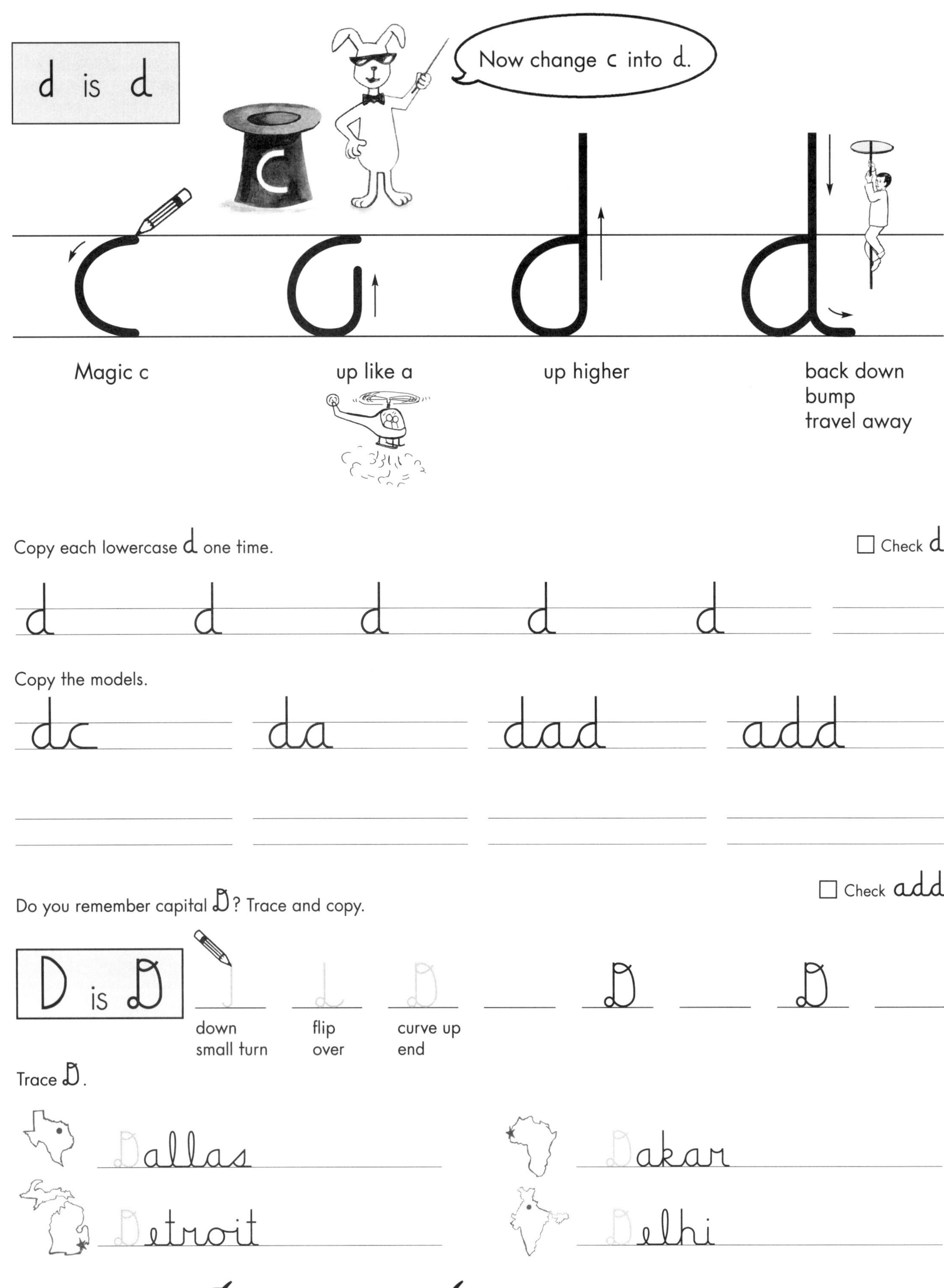

Copy each lowercase d one time.

☐ Check d

d   d   d   d   d

Copy the models.

dc   da   dad   add

☐ Check add

Do you remember capital D? Trace and copy.

Trace D.

Dallas   Dakar

Detroit   Delhi

▮ Check word.   Teachers: Help children ✔ their letter for correct size, placement, and connections.

    © 2022 Learning Without Tears

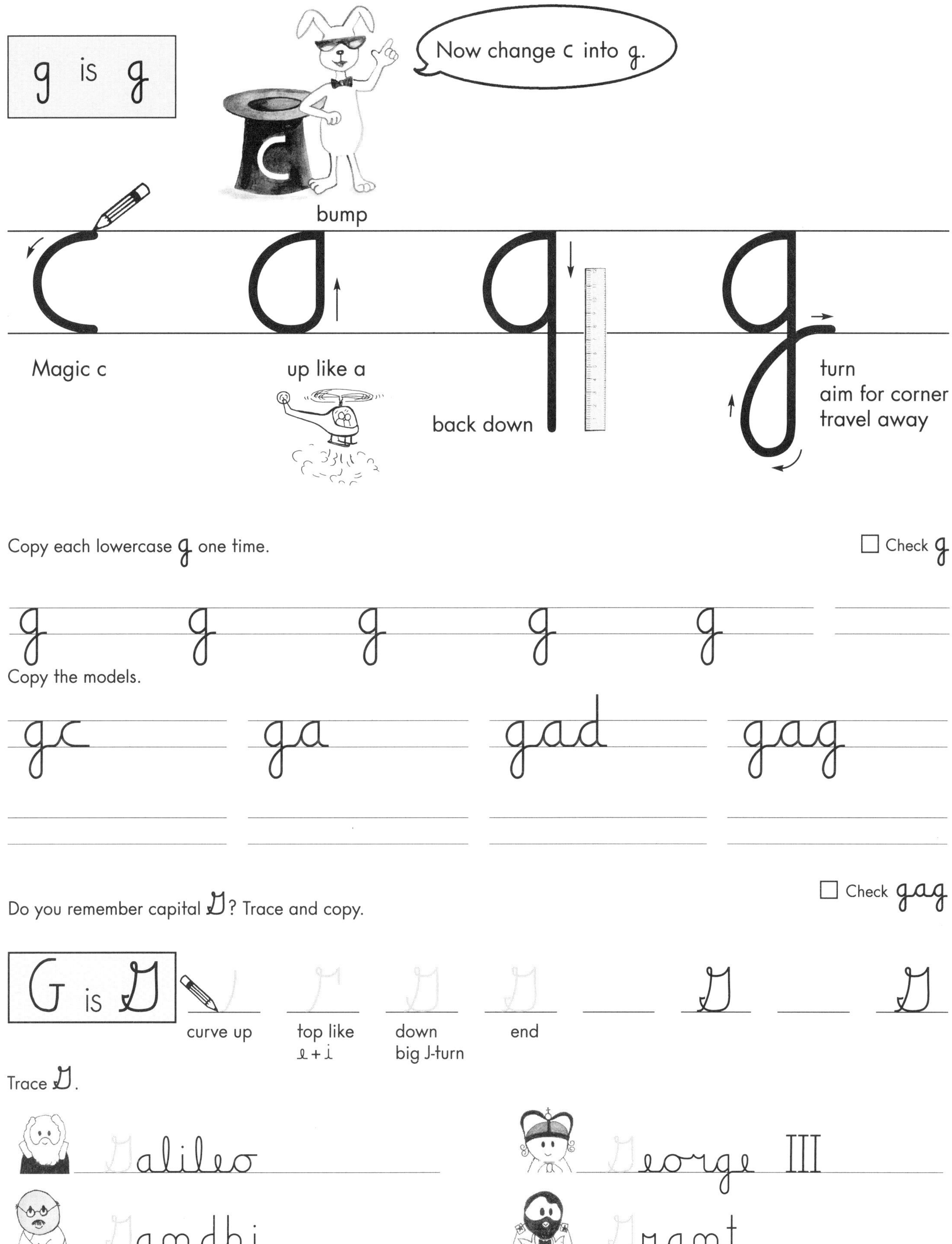

Copy each lowercase g one time. ☐ Check g

g   g   g   g   g

Copy the models.

gc   ga   gad   gag

☐ Check gag

Do you remember capital G? Trace and copy.

G is G
curve up
top like ℓ + i
down big J-turn
end

Trace G.

Galileo   George III

Gandhi   Grant

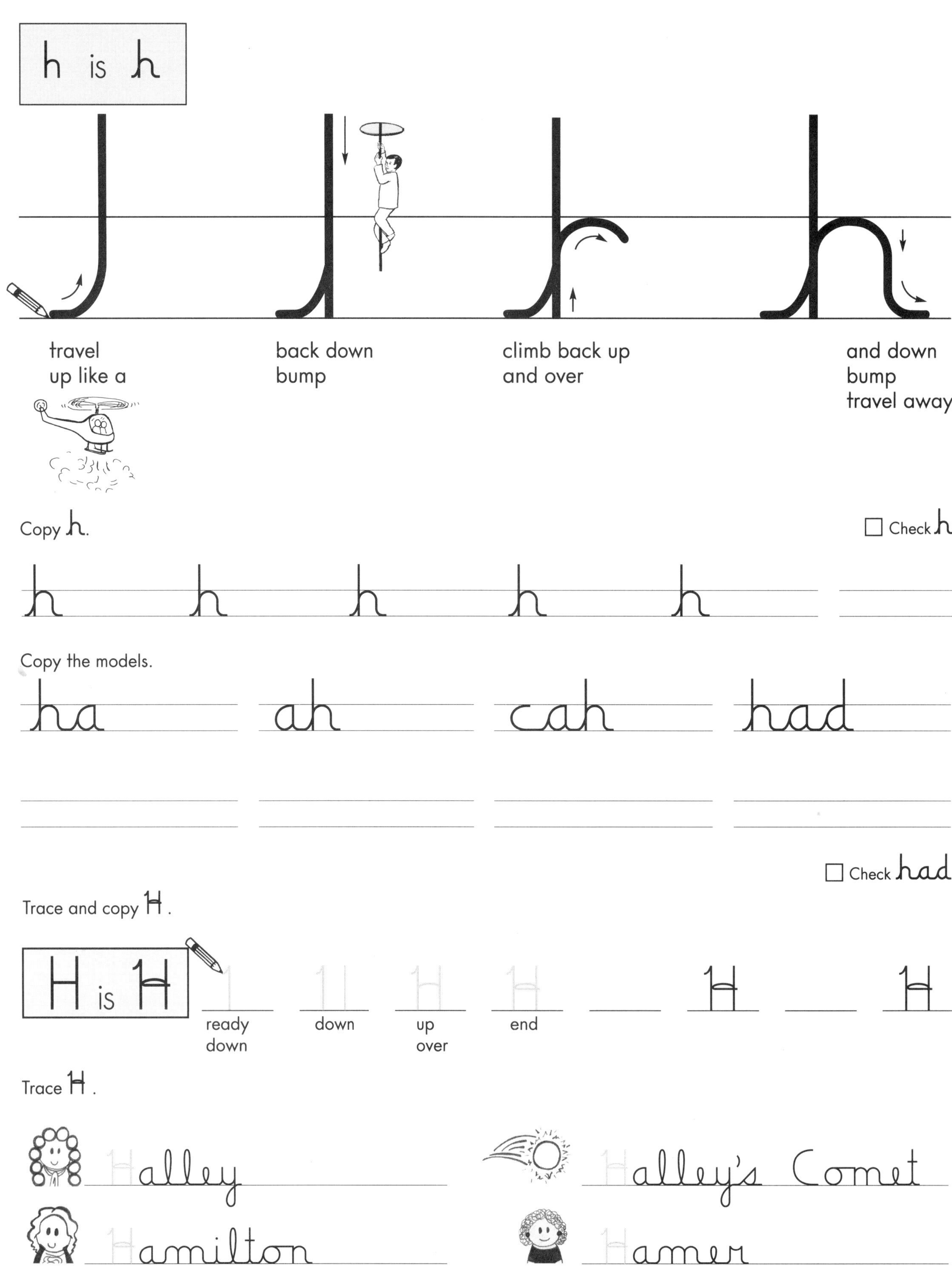

h is h
travel
up like a
back down
bump
climb back up
and over
and down
bump
travel away
Copy h.
Check h
Copy the models.
ha
ah
cah
had
Check had
Trace and copy H.
H is H
ready
down
down
up
over
end
Trace H.
Halley
Halley's Comet
Hamilton
Hamer

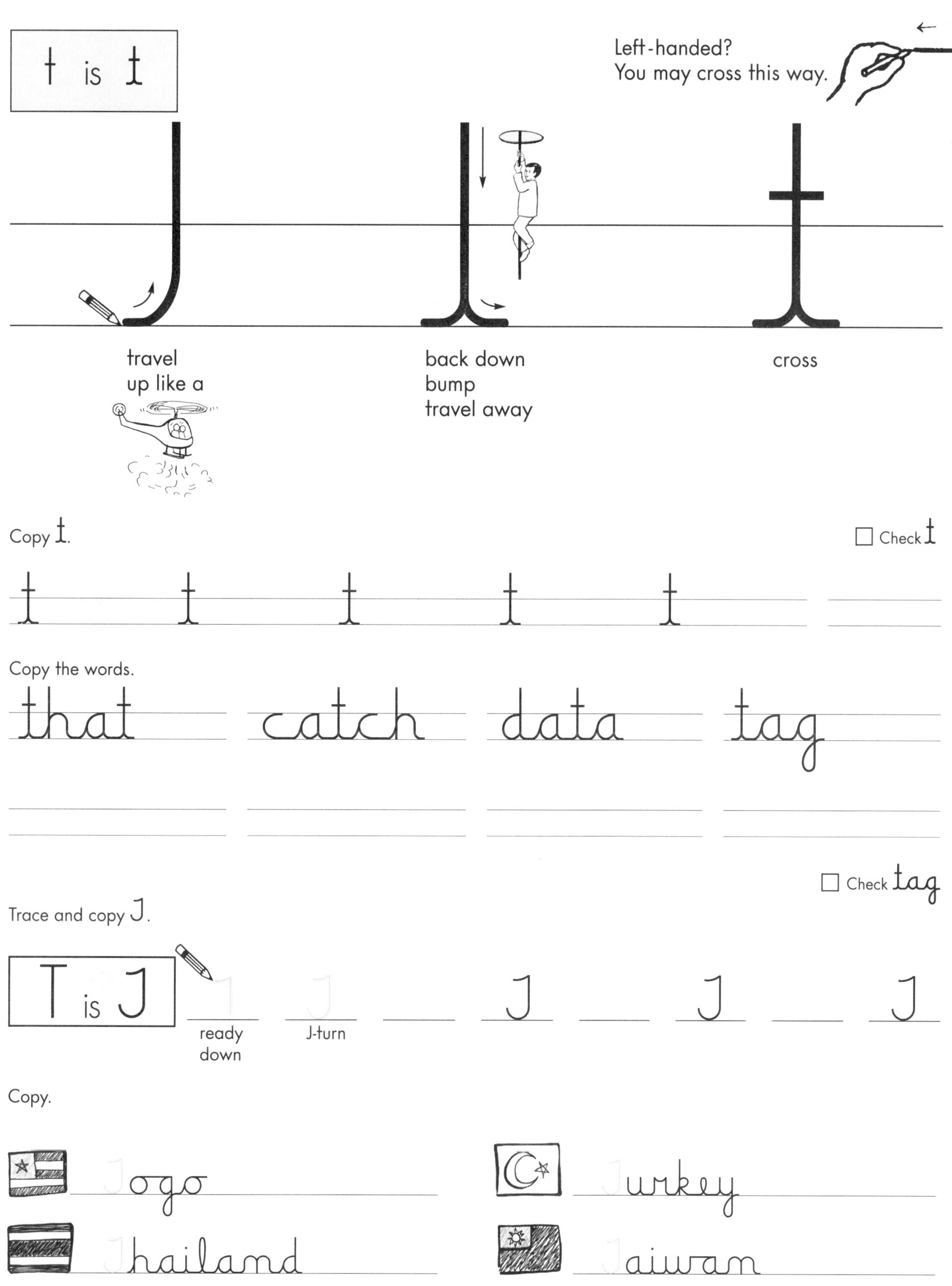

t is t

Left-handed?
You may cross this way.

travel
up like a

back down
bump
travel away

cross

Copy t.   ☐ Check t

Copy the words.

that   catch   data   tag

☐ Check tag

Trace and copy J.

T is J

ready
down

J-turn

Copy.

Togo

Turkey

Thailand

Taiwan

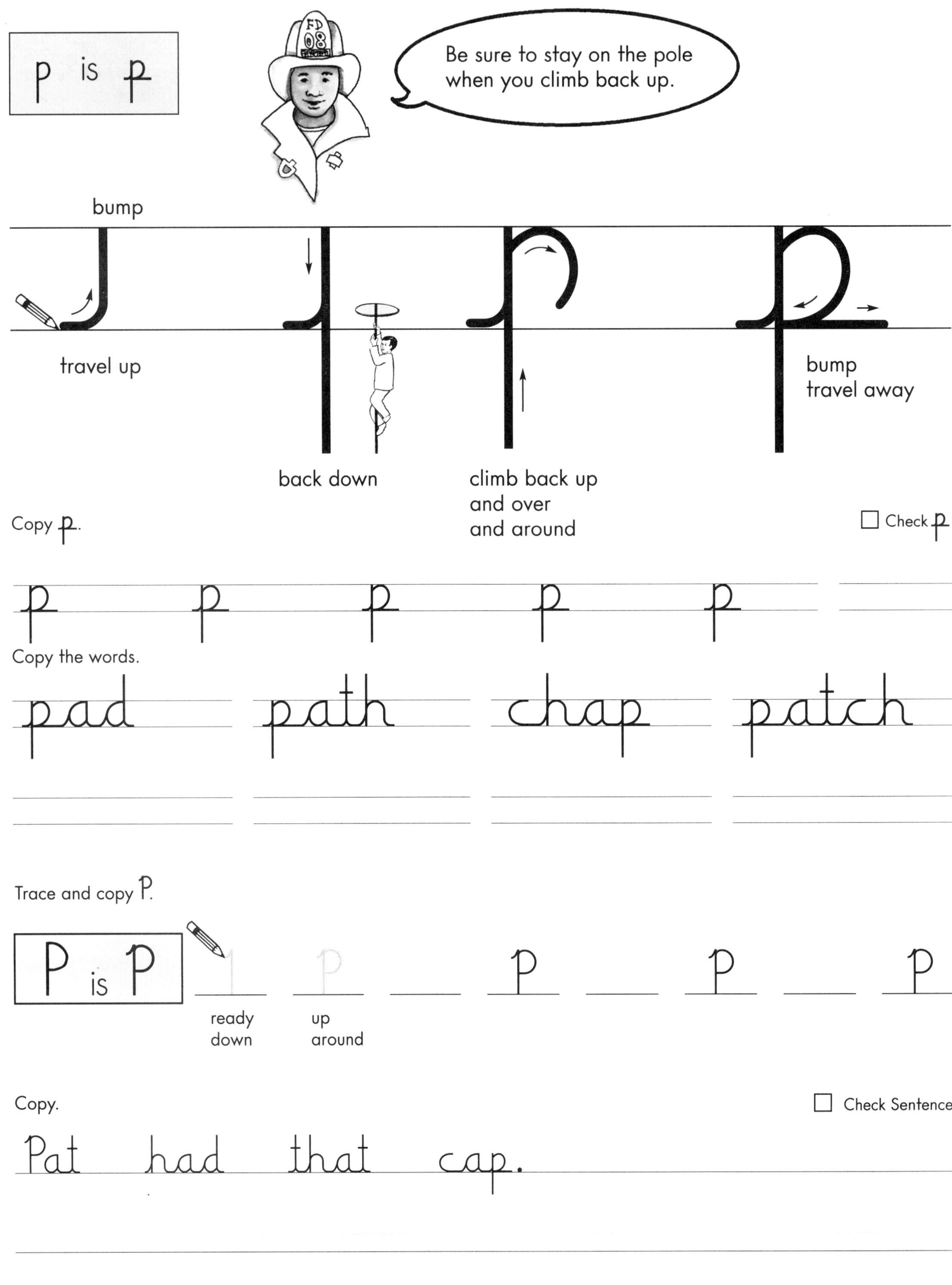

Copy p.   ☐ Check p

Copy the words.

pad   path   chap   patch

Trace and copy P.

P   P   P   P

Copy.   ☐ Check Sentence

Pat had that cap.

Check sentence.   Teachers: Help children ✔ their sentence for correct capitalization, word spacing, and ending punctuation.

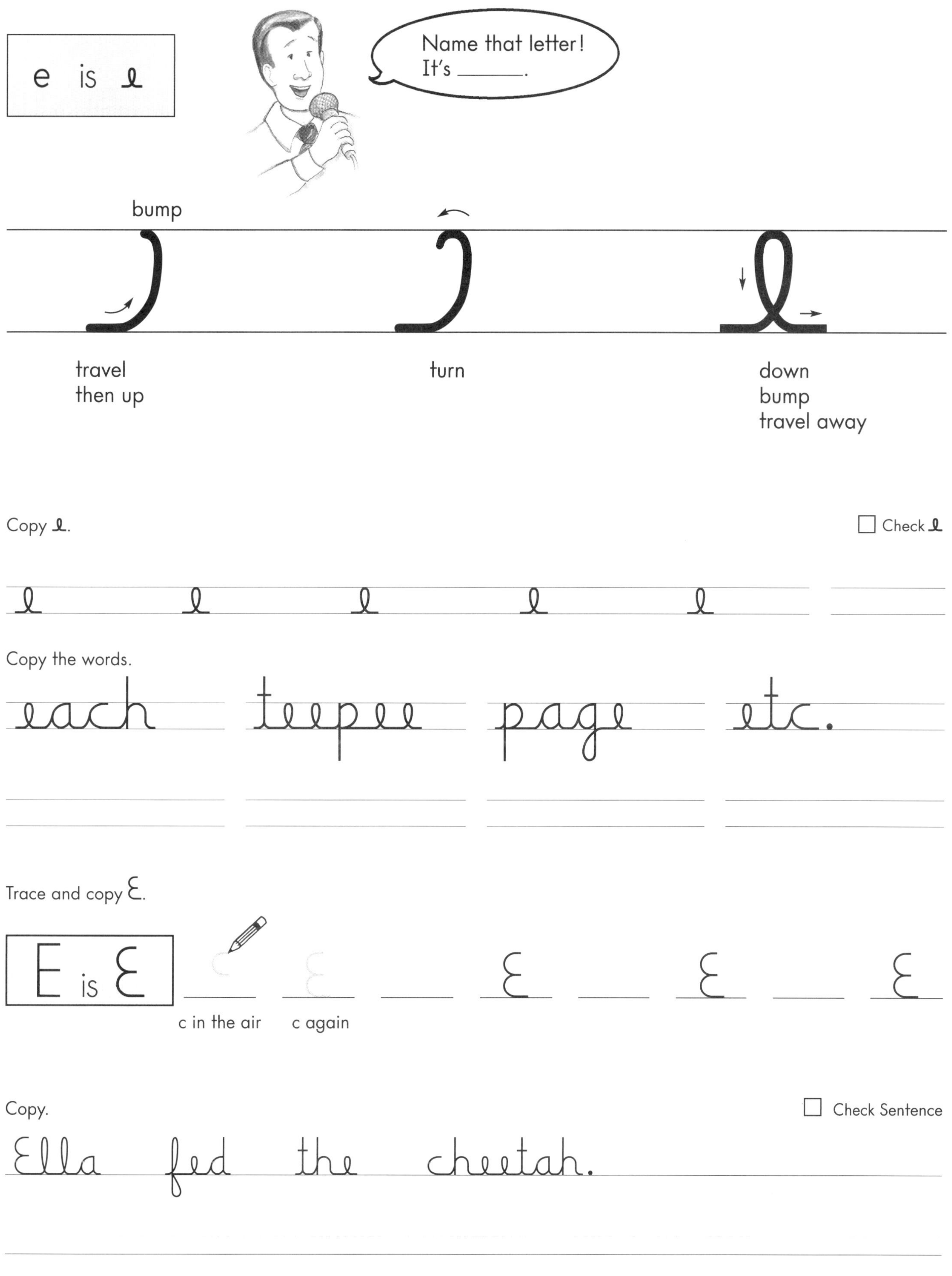

e is ℓ
Name that letter! It's _______.
bump
travel then up
turn
down bump travel away
Copy ℓ.
Check ℓ
Copy the words.
each   teepee   page   etc.
Trace and copy Ɛ.
E is Ɛ
c in the air   c again
Copy.
Check Sentence
Ella fed the cheetah.

l is *l*

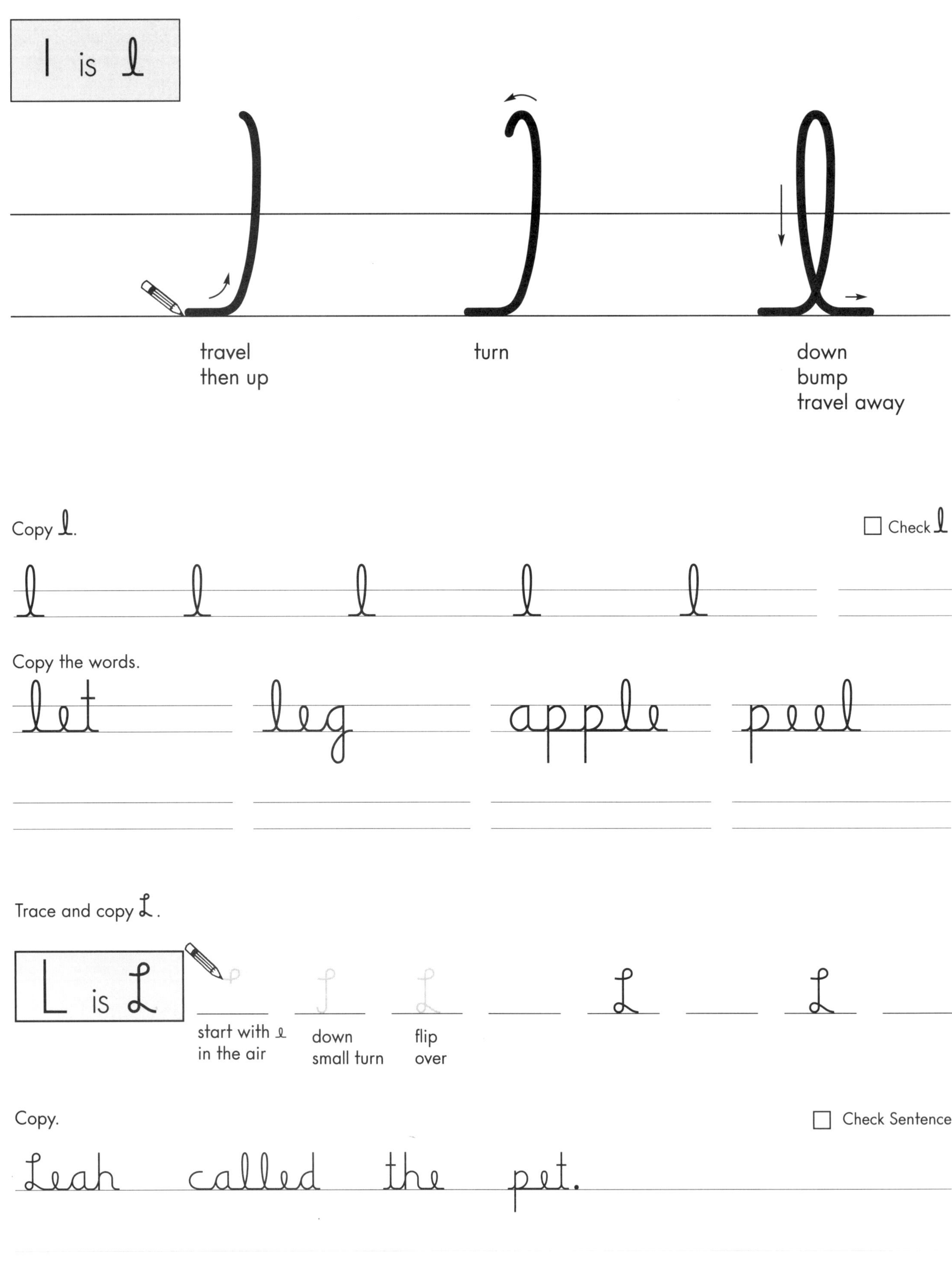

Copy *l*.

☐ Check *l*

Copy the words.

let   leg   apple   peel

Trace and copy *L*.

L is *L*

Copy.

☐ Check Sentence

Leah called the pet.

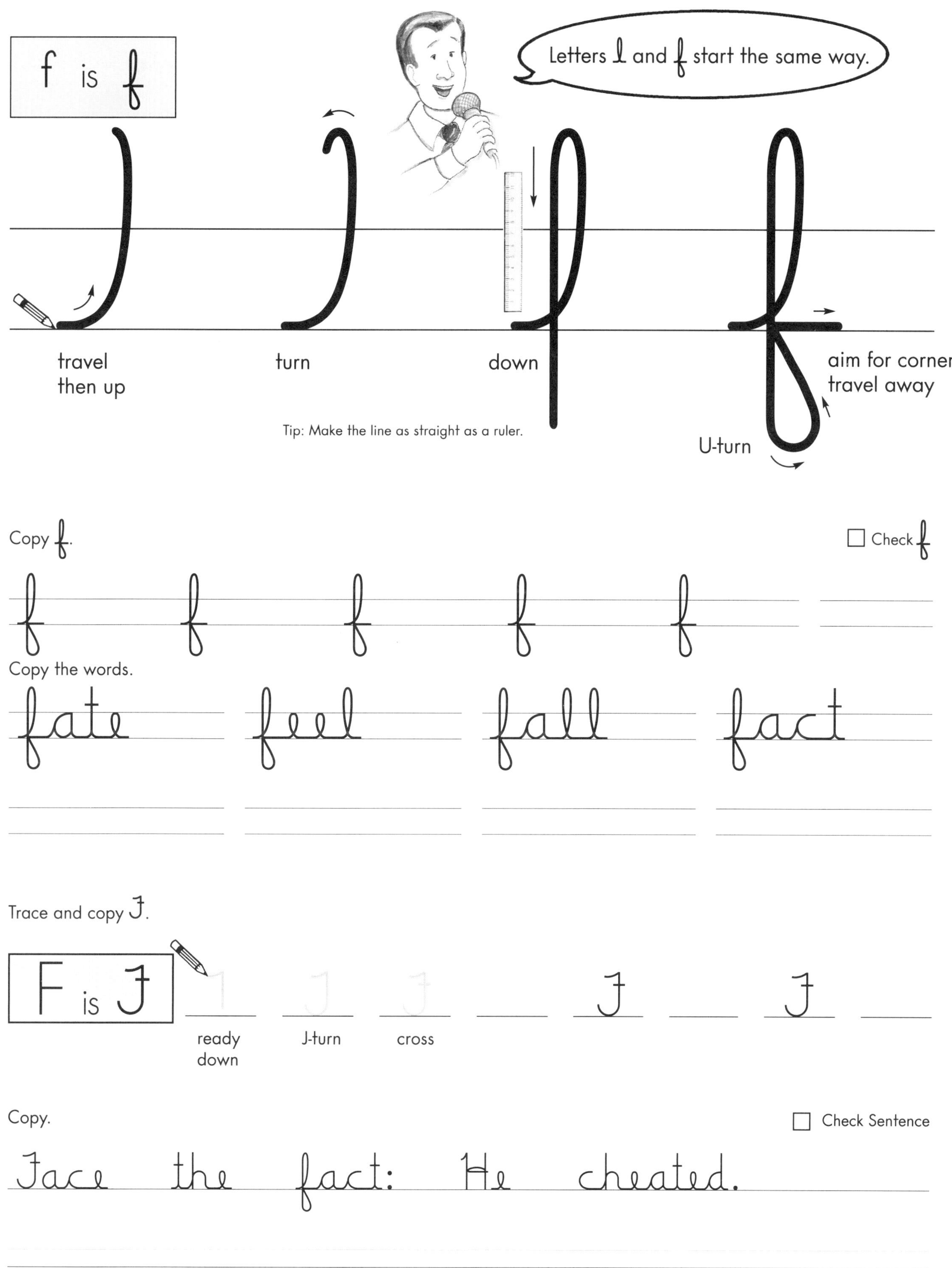

f is f
Letters l and f start the same way.
travel then up
turn
down
aim for corner travel away
U-turn
Tip: Make the line as straight as a ruler.
Copy f.
Check f
Copy the words.
fate   feel   fall   fact
Trace and copy F.
F is F
ready down
J-turn
cross
Copy.
Check Sentence
Face the fact: He cheated.

a b c d e f g h i j k l m
n o p q r s t u v w x y z

Wait for the teacher to play the Freeze Game.

call — called

eat — ate

—

—

heat — heated

lead — led

—

—

help — helped

feel — felt

—

—

place — placed

fall — fell

—

—

tag — tagged

feed — fed

—

—

Wait for the teacher to spell the words. Write the words in cursive.

Translate print into cursive.

1. a
2. at
3. cap
4. flag
5. place
6. called
7. fetched
8. accepted
9. delegated
10. tattletale

1.
2.
3.
4.
5.
6.
7.
8.
9.
10.

u is u

tug

bump

down
travel up

back down
bump
travel away

Copy u. ☐ Check u

u u u u u

Copy the words.

up tug glue laugh

Trace and copy U.

U is U

down
travel, up

back
down

U U U

Copy. ☐ Check Sentence

Ulla laughed at Ed.

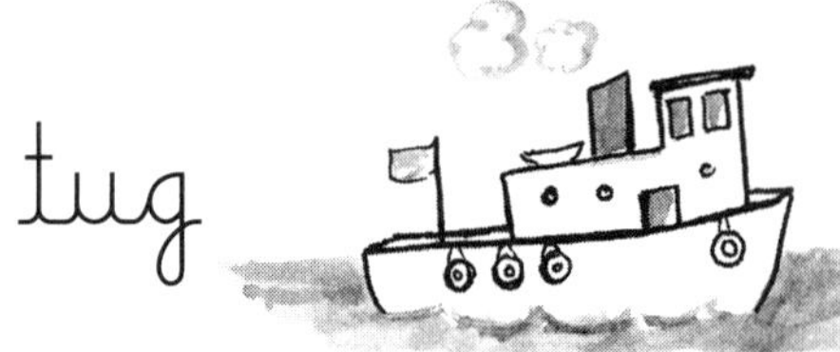

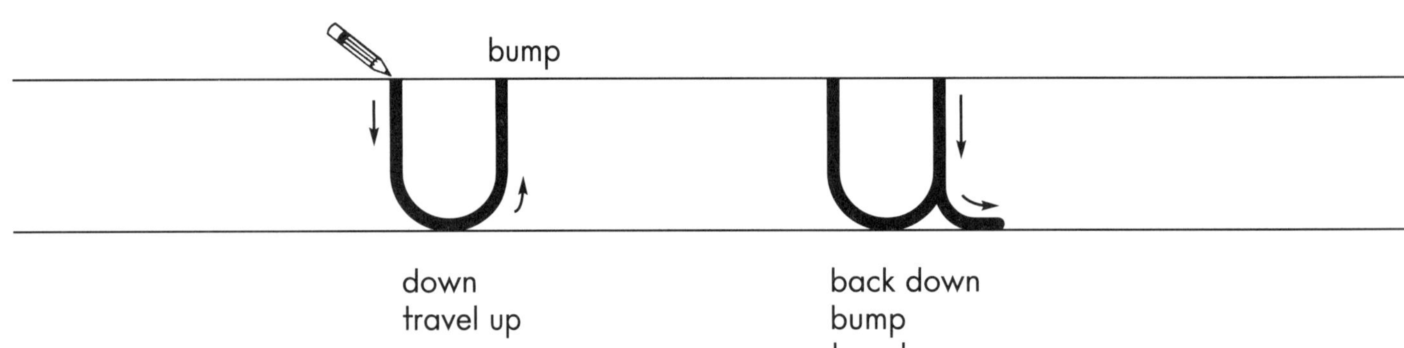

y is y

eye

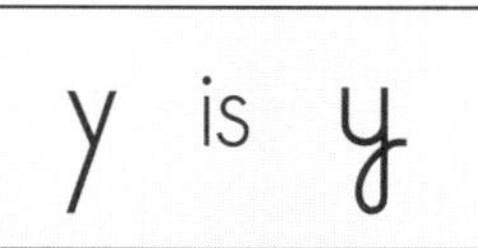

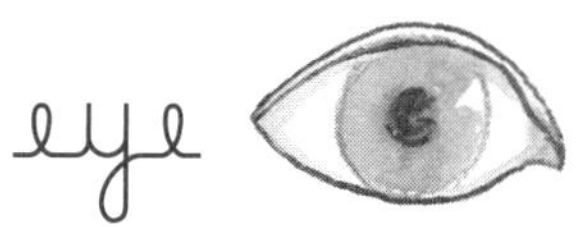

bump
Make the line as straight as a ruler.
down
travel up
back down
turn
aim for corner
travel away

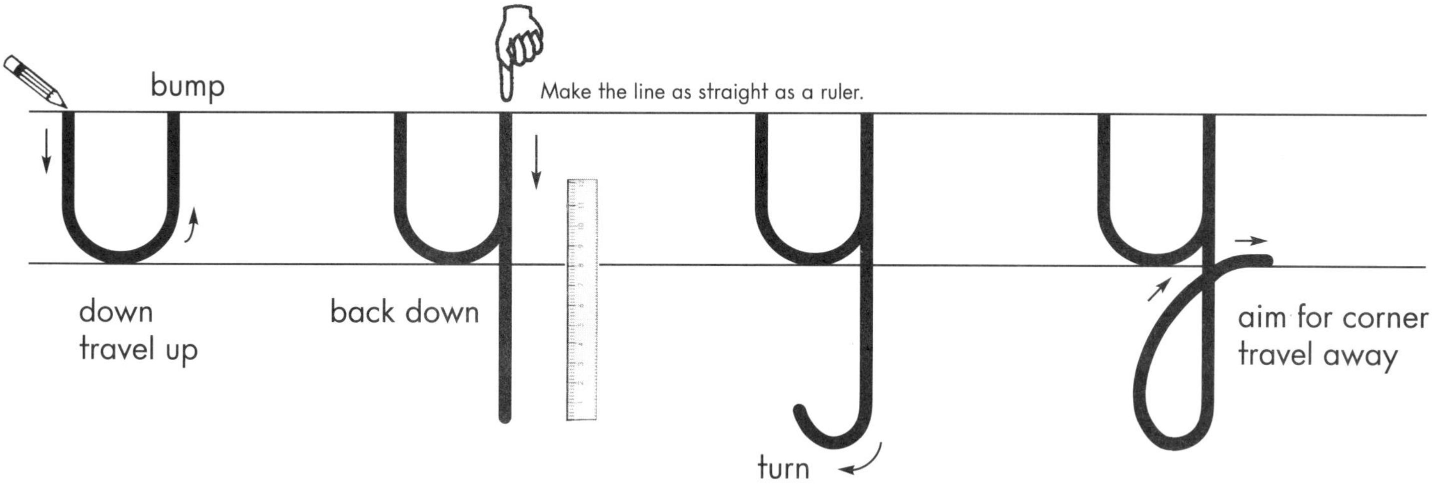

Copy y. ☐ Check y

y y y y y

Copy the words.

yell yet fly eye

Trace and copy y.

Y is y

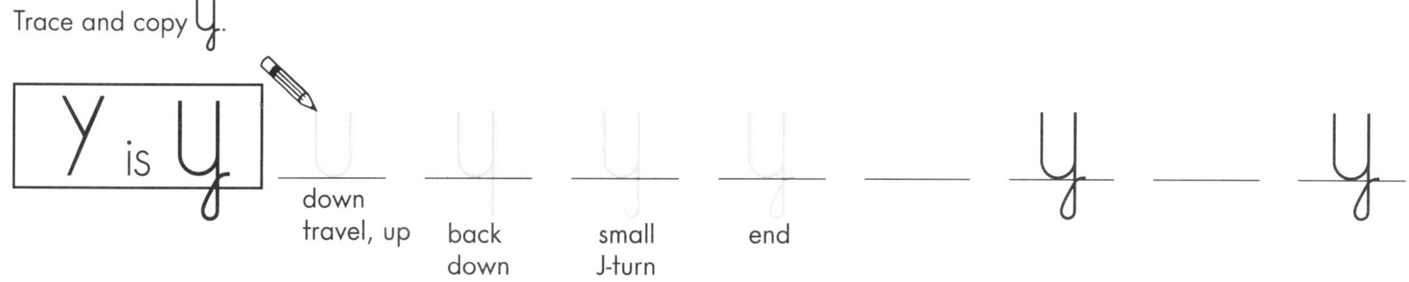

down travel, up | back down | small J-turn | end

y y

Copy. ☐ Check Sentence

Yul yelled, "Help Ada!"

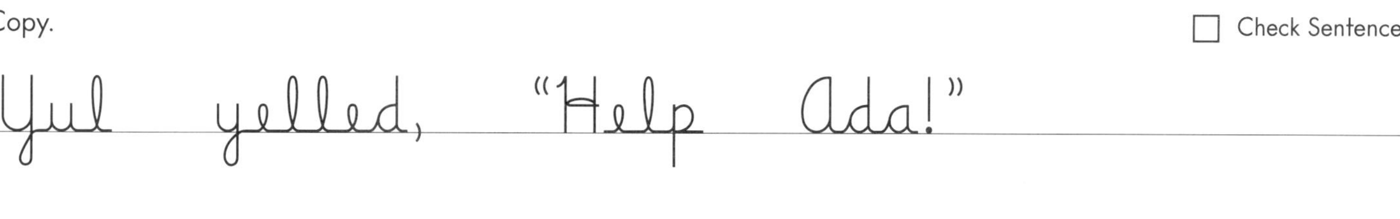

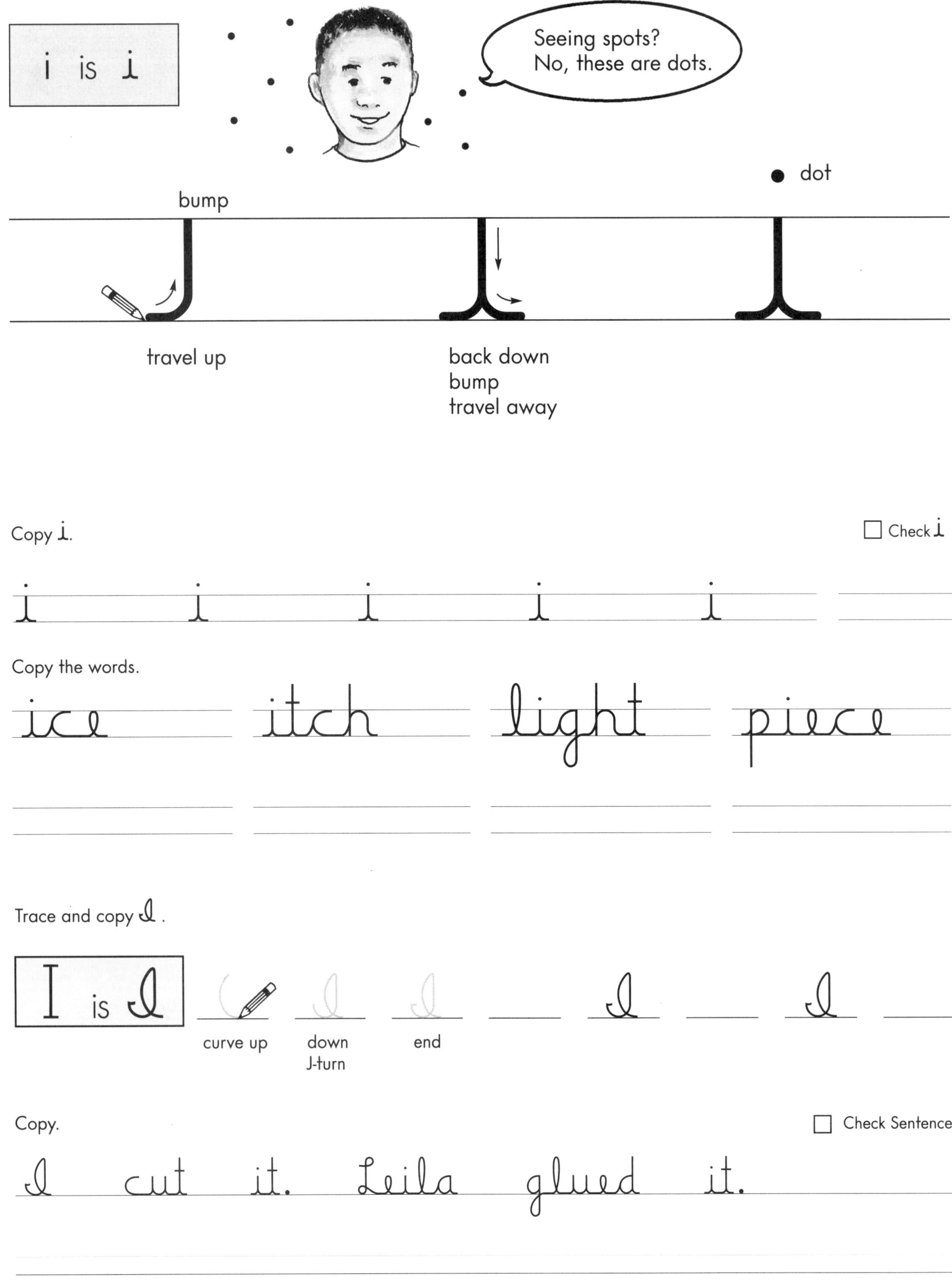

Copy i. ☐ Check i

i   i   i   i   i

Copy the words.

ice   itch   light   piece

Trace and copy I.

Copy. ☐ Check Sentence

I cut it. Leila glued it.

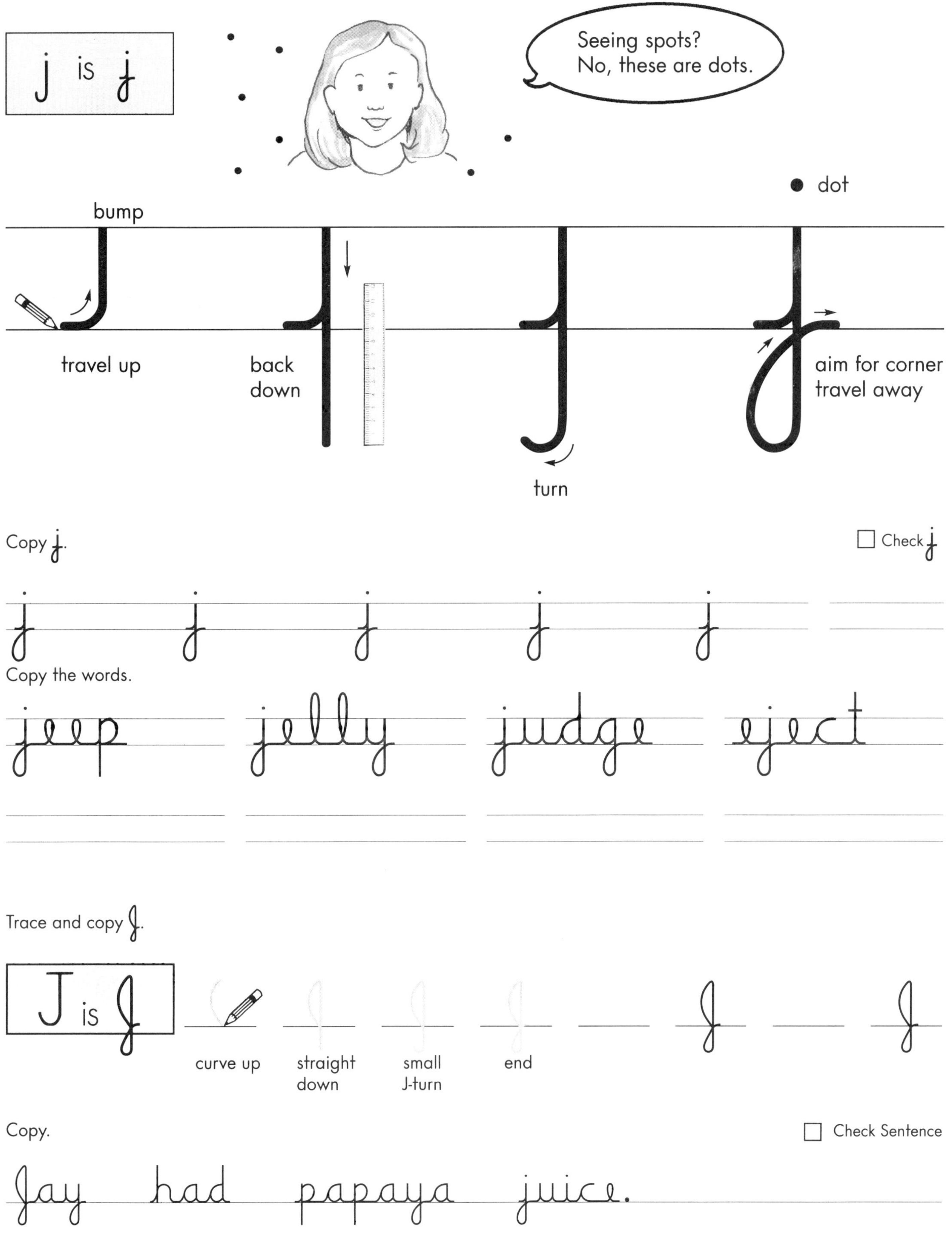

Copy j.

Check j

Copy the words.

jeep   jelly   judge   eject

Trace and copy J.

J is J

curve up   straight down   small J-turn   end

Copy.

Check Sentence

Jay had papaya juice.

Cursive Success **23**

a b c d e f g h **i** **j** k l m
n o p q r s t **u** v w x **y** z

Wait for the teacher to play the Freeze Game.

dig - dug

catch - caught

teach - taught

put - put

hide - hid

Cursive with new letters: i j u y

pay - paid

hit - hit

pull - pulled

yell - yelled

update - updated

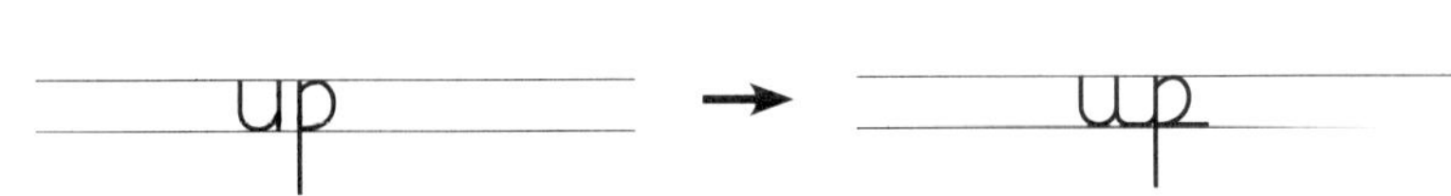

Wait for the teacher to spell the words.
Write the words in cursive.

Translate print into cursive.

1. u i y j
2. up
3. fit
4. jeep
5. eight
6. played
7. delight
8. actually
9. difficult
10. delightful

1.
2.
3.
4.
5.
6.
7.
8.
9.
10.

k is k
kite
travel
up like a
back down
bump
climb back up
and over
and around
kick!
slide down
travel away
Copy k.
Check k
Copy the words.
kite   kettle   talk   picky
Trace and copy K.
K is K
ready
down
kick!
slide
down
Copy.
Check Sentence
Kate picked up the kit.

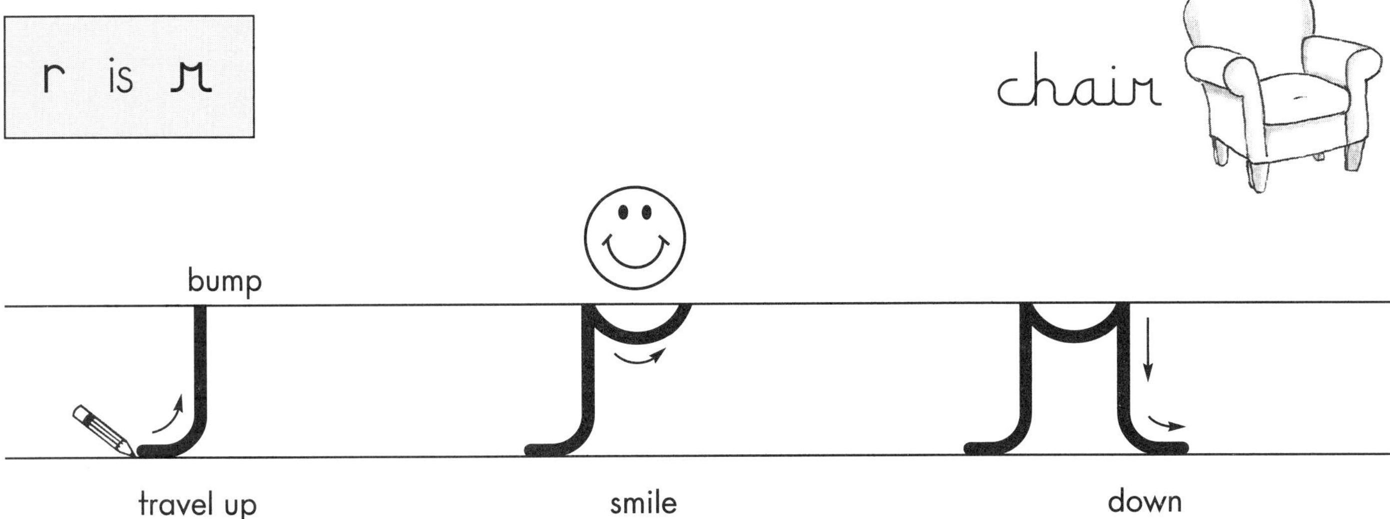

r is r

chair

Copy r.

☐ Check r

r r r r r

Copy the words.

raft radar their there

Trace and copy R.

R is R

ready down

up around

slide down

R R

Copy.

☐ Check Sentence

Rachel, are they ready?

s is _s_

sail

bump

straight jet takeoff

down
make a J-turn

bump
travel away

Copy each lowercase _s_ one time.

☐ Check _s_

Copy the words.

she *sure* *sail* *last*

Trace and copy _S_.

S is _S_

straight
jet takeoff

print S

end

Copy.

☐ Check Sentence

Sharks' teeth are sharp.

28 *Cursive Success*

© 2022 Learning Without Tears

Add _s_ to make plural nouns.

boat   skate   ball   boot

Rewrite the sentences with the new subjects. Add _s_ to verbs to make them agree with the subjects.

They sail.	He sails.
I agree.	He
You talk.	She
We read.	Ben
You sleep.	Ava
They laugh.	David

Review & Mastery: Cursive to Cursive

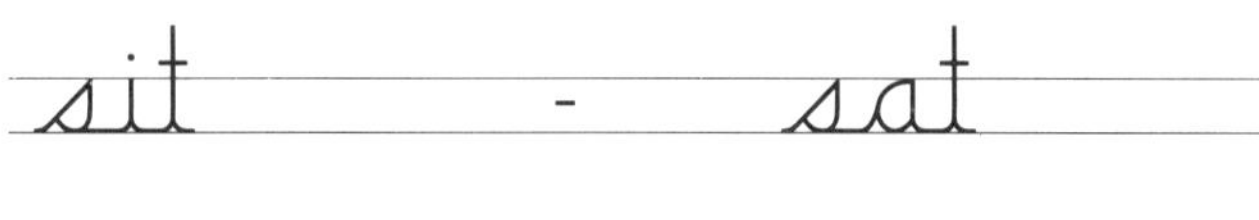

Wait for the teacher to play the Freeze Game.

Cursive with new letters: k r s

sit - sat	fry - fried
keep - kept	hear - heard
say - said	sleep - slept
read - read	speed - sped
try - tried	shut - shut

Wait for the teacher to spell the words. Write the words in cursive.

Translate print into cursive.

1. k r s

2. as

3. kid

4. park

5. skate

6. repeat

7. traffic

8. straight

9. scratched

10. artificial

1.

2.

3.

4.

5.

6.

7.

8.

9.

10.

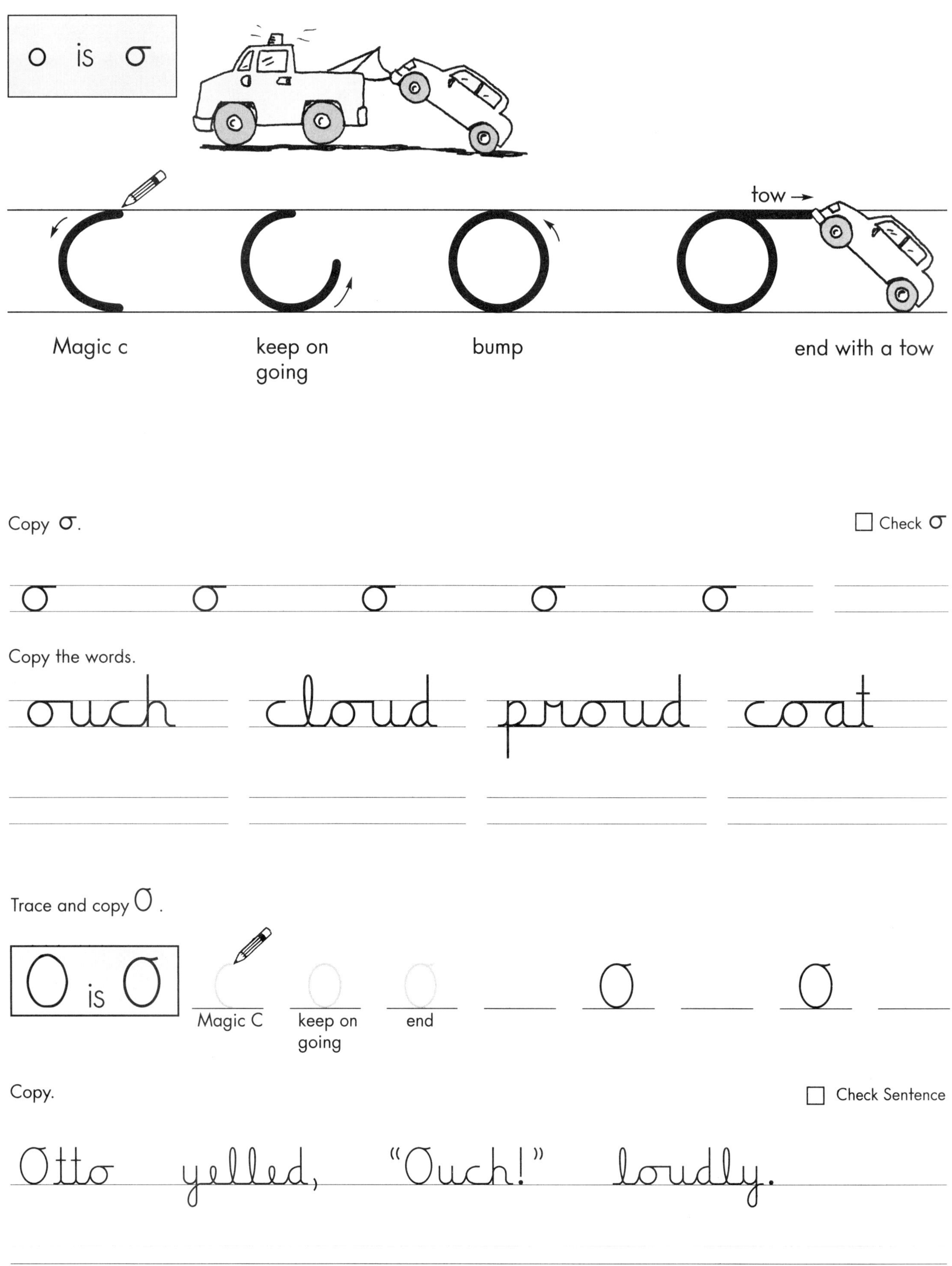

Copy σ. ☐ Check σ

Copy the words.

ouch   cloud   proud   coat

Trace and copy O.

Copy. ☐ Check Sentence

Otto yelled, "Ouch!" loudly.

Tricky Connections – after σ

Crank us up to tow us.

Copy the models.

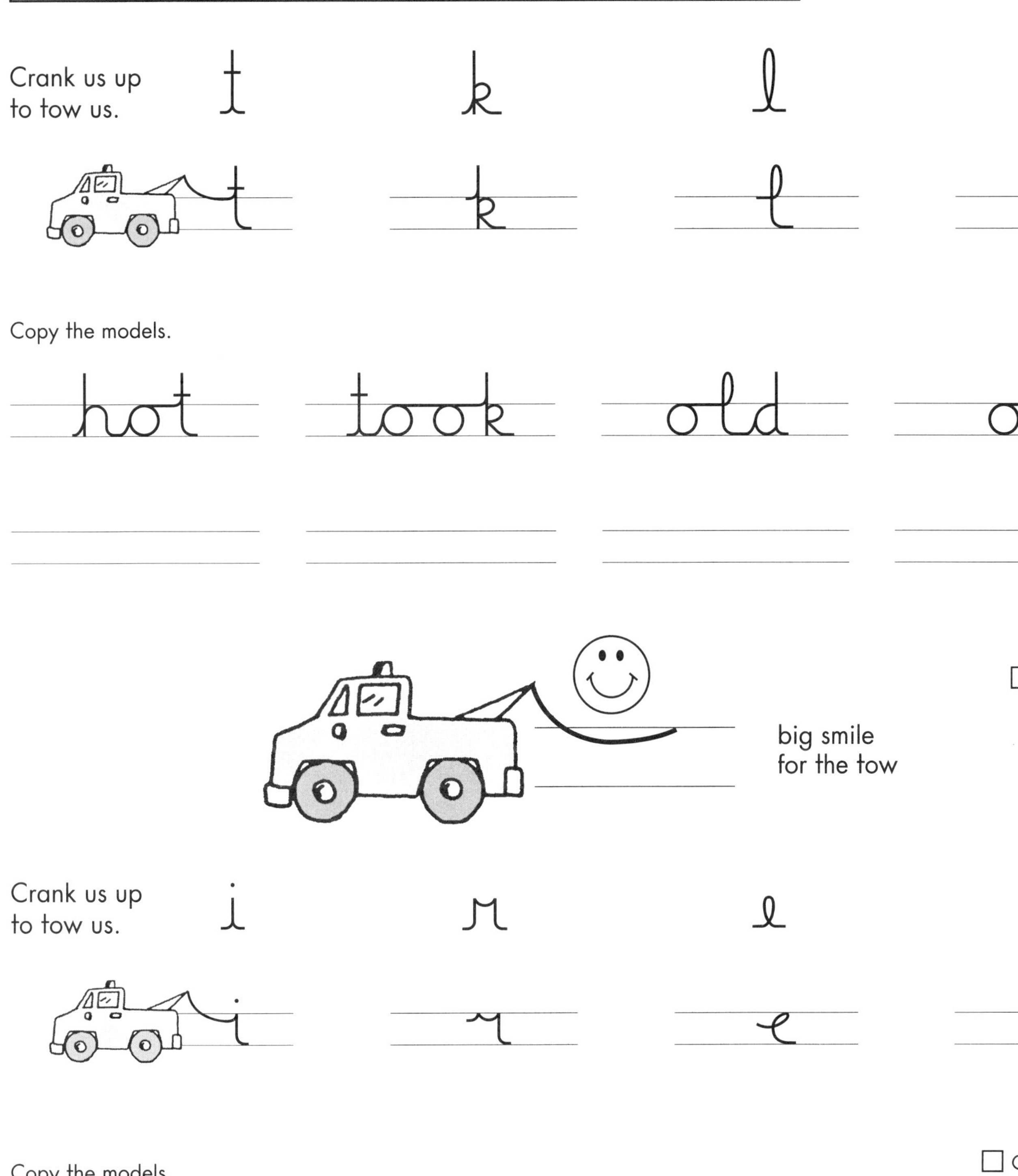

big smile
for the tow

☐ Check of

Crank us up to tow us.

☐ Check lost

Copy the models.

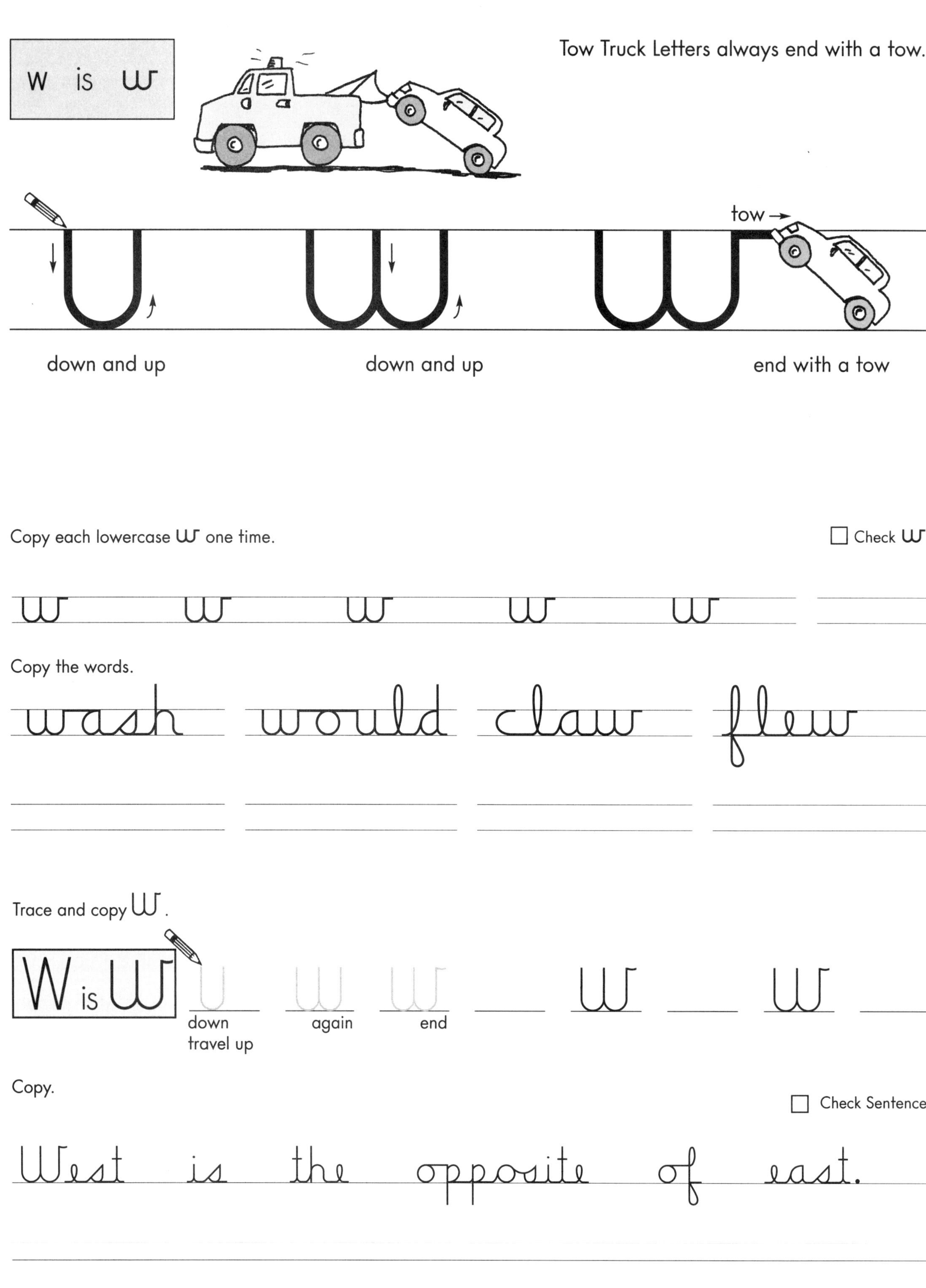

Copy each lowercase w one time.   ☐ Check w

Copy the words.

wash   would   claw   flew

Trace and copy w.

Copy.   ☐ Check Sentence

West is the opposite of east.

Tricky Connections – after 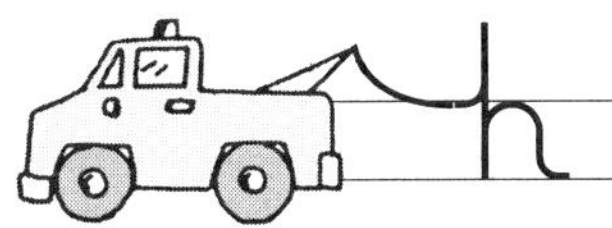

Crank us up to tow us.

Copy the models.

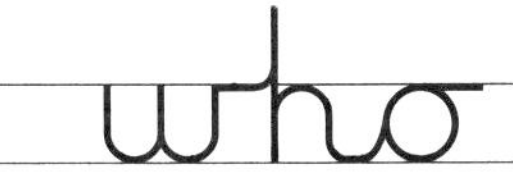who 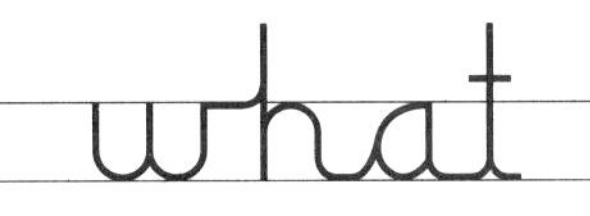what where 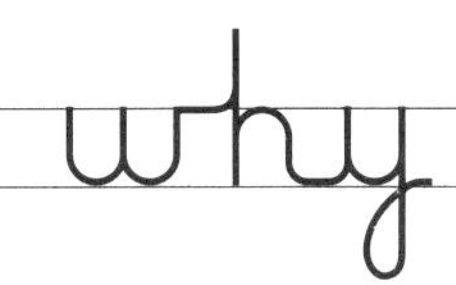why

☐ Check why

Crank us up to tow us.

☐ Check jaws

Copy the models.

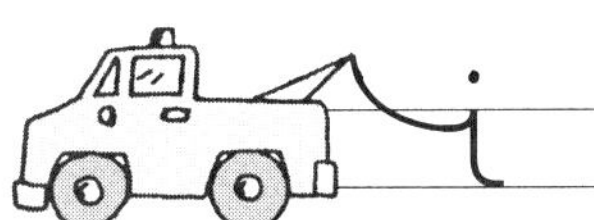wish write we jaws

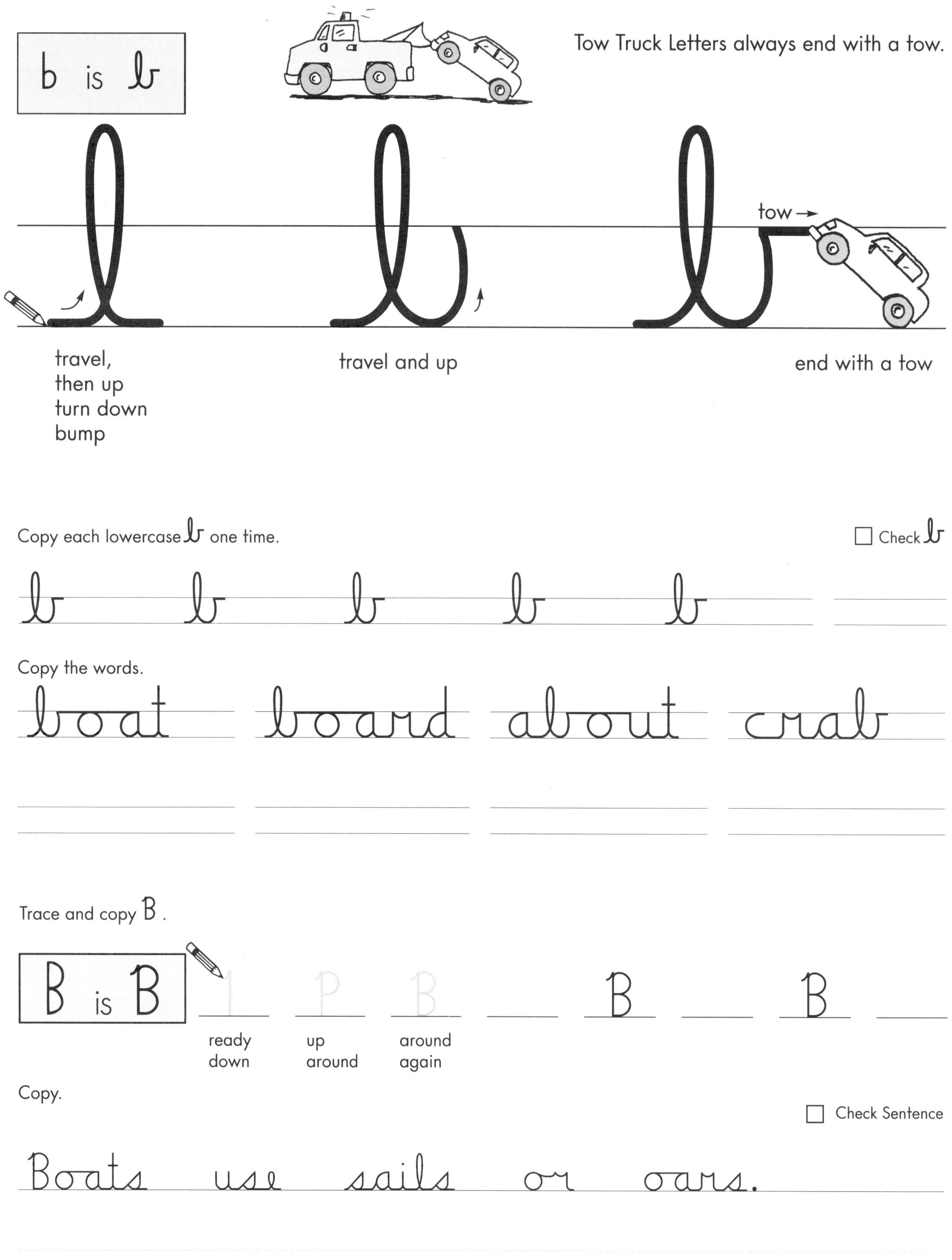

b is ℔

Tow Truck Letters always end with a tow.

tow →

travel,
then up
turn down
bump

travel and up

end with a tow

Copy each lowercase ℔ one time.　☐ Check ℔

Copy the words.

boat　*board*　*about*　*crab*

Trace and copy B.

B is B

ready
down

up
around

around
again

Copy.　☐ Check Sentence

Boats use sails or oars.

Crank us up to tow us.

Copy the models.

 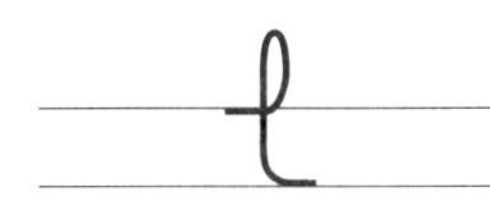 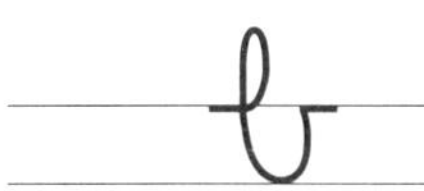 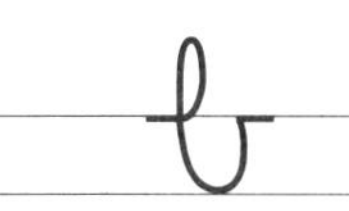

  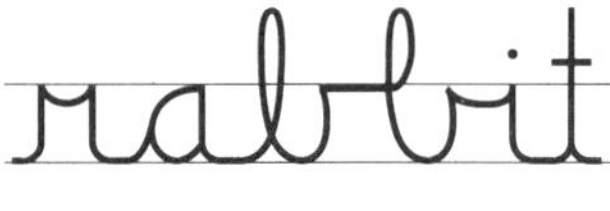 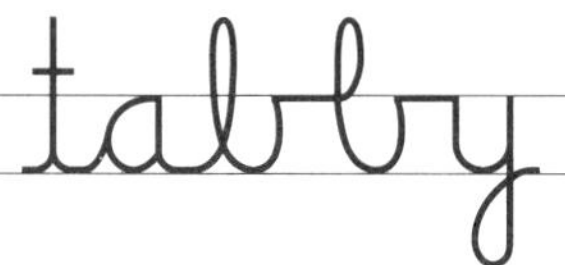

□ Check _tabby_

big smile
for the tow

Crank us up to tow us.

□ Check _tubs_

Copy the models.

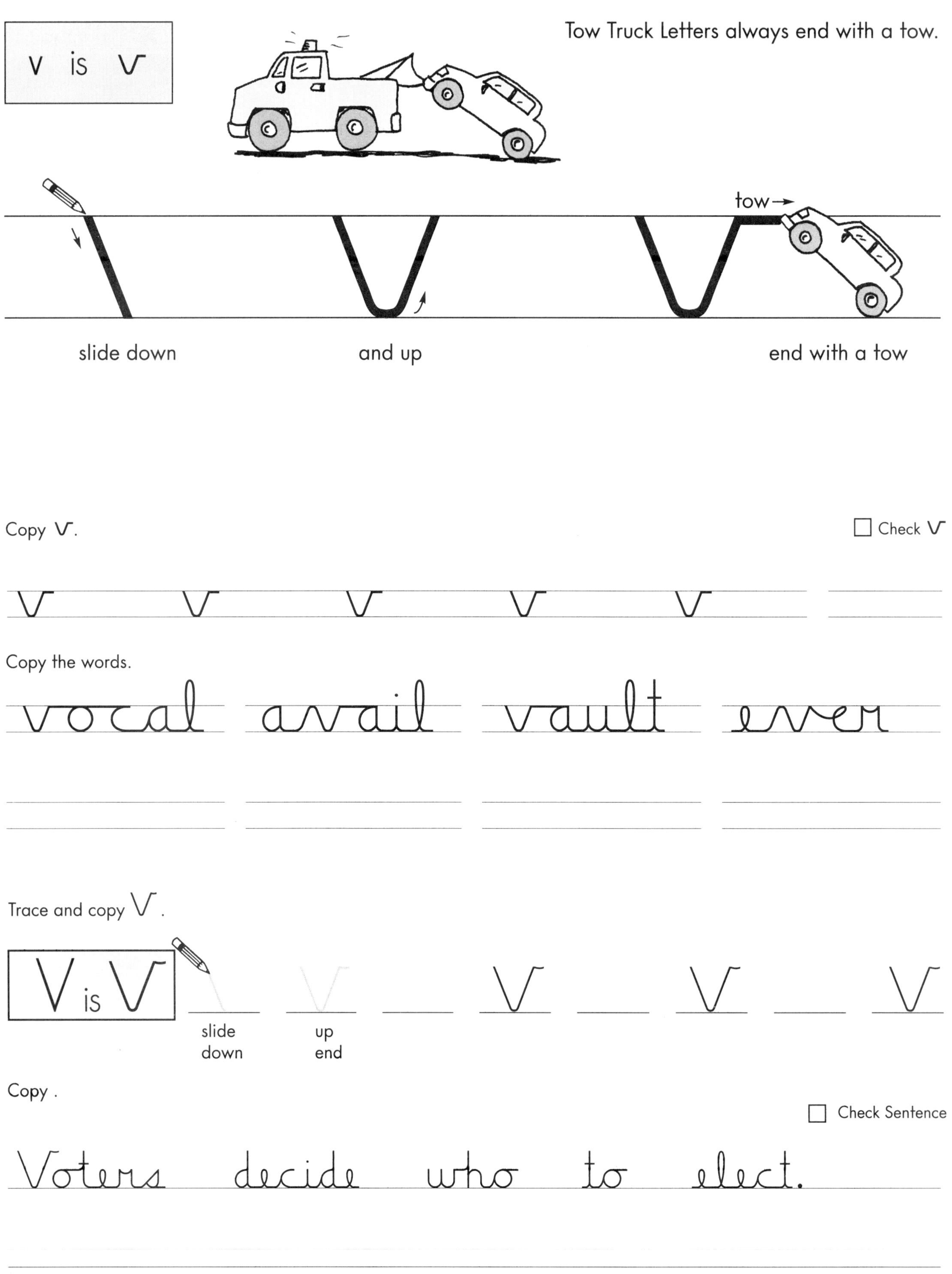

V is V

Copy V.   ☐ Check V

Copy the words.

vocal   avail   vault   ever

Trace and copy V.

V is V

slide
down
up
end

Copy.   ☐ Check Sentence

Voters decide who to elect.

Tricky Connections – after ∨

Crank us up
to tow us.

Copy the models.

very   verb   save   have

☐ Check **have**

Crank us up
to tow us.

☐ Check **virus**

Copy the models.

vice   video   view   virus

a b c d e f g h i j k l m
n o p q r s t u v w x y z

Wait for the teacher to play the Freeze Game.

Cursive with new letters: b o v w

ride — rode

fight — fought

tell — told

take — took

is — was

buy — bought

hold — held

shake — shook

give — gave

sell — sold

Spelling to Cursive

be → be

Wait for the teacher to spell the words.
Write the words in cursive.

Translate print into cursive.

1. o w b v
2. be
3. bus
4. echo
5. jewel
6. driver
7. hopeful
8. football
9. beautiful
10. vocabulary

1.
2.
3.
4.
5.
6.
7.
8.
9.
10.

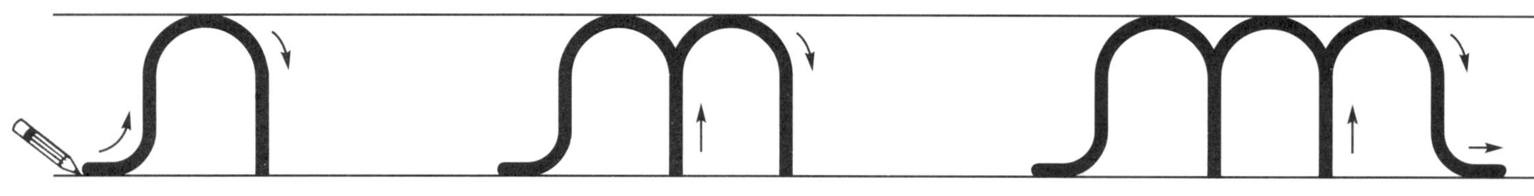

travel
up and over
down

up and over
down

again
travel away

Copy 𝓂 .   ☐ Check 𝓂

Copy the words.

me   them   him   mule

Trace and copy m .

M is m _____ _____ _____ m _____ m _____

ready
down

up, over
down

again

Copy .   ☐ Check Sentence

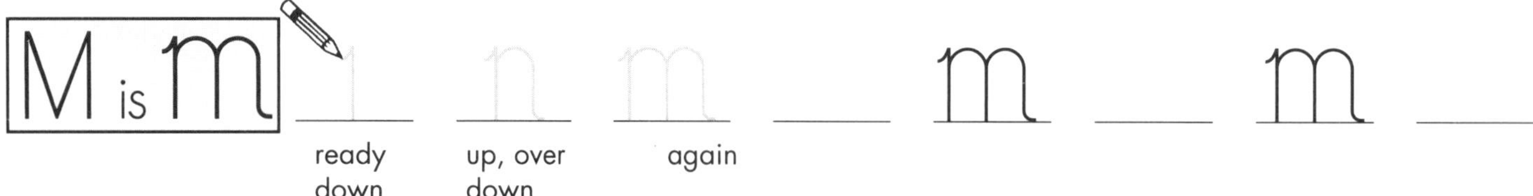

Morning   is   when   birds   sing.

After a Tow Truck Letter, use **printed** m.

Copy m .　　　　　　　　　　　　　　　　　□ Check m

m　　　　m　　　　m　　　　m

Copy the words.

come　　　　　come

prom　　　　　prom

from　　　　　from

some　　　　　some

home　　　　　home

□ Check home

n is m or n

violin

travel
up and over
down

again
travel away

Copy m.

☐ Check m

Copy the words.

not   night   know   violin

Trace and copy n.

N is n

ready
down

up, over
down

Copy .

☐ Check Sentence

Night is when bats fly.

SPECIAL SITUATION

After a Tow Truck Letter, use **printed** n.

Copy n.　　　　　　　　　　　　　　　　　□ Check n

n　　n　　n　　n　　n

Copy the words.

only　　　　　　only

once　　　　　　once

own　　　　　　own

front　　　　　　front

brown　　　　　　brown

□ Check brown

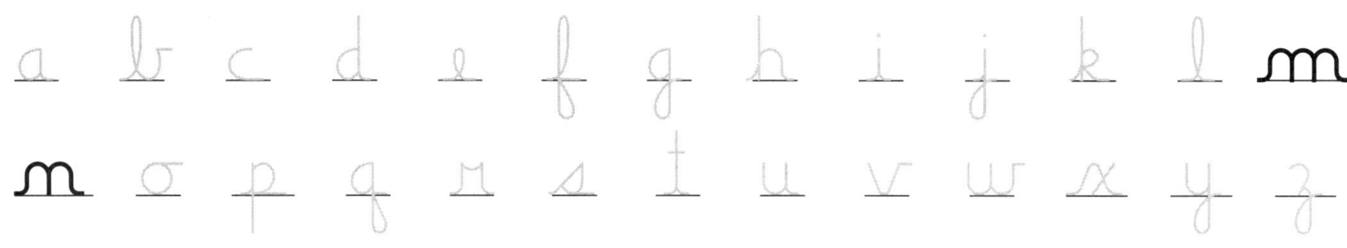

Cursive with new letters: m m

Wait for the teacher to play the Freeze Game.

sing - sang

come - came

shine - shone

ring - rang

go - went

know - knew

win - won

make - made

spend - spent

spin - spun

<table>
<tr><td>

Print to Cursive

Translate print into cursive.

1. m n

2. my

3. man

4. navy

5. nature

6. saving

7. machine

8. interest

9. submarine

10. navigation

</td><td>

Spelling to Cursive

Wait for the teacher to spell the words.
Write the words in cursive.

1.

2.

3.

4.

5.

6.

7.

8.

9.

10.

</td></tr>
</table>

Cursive Success **47**

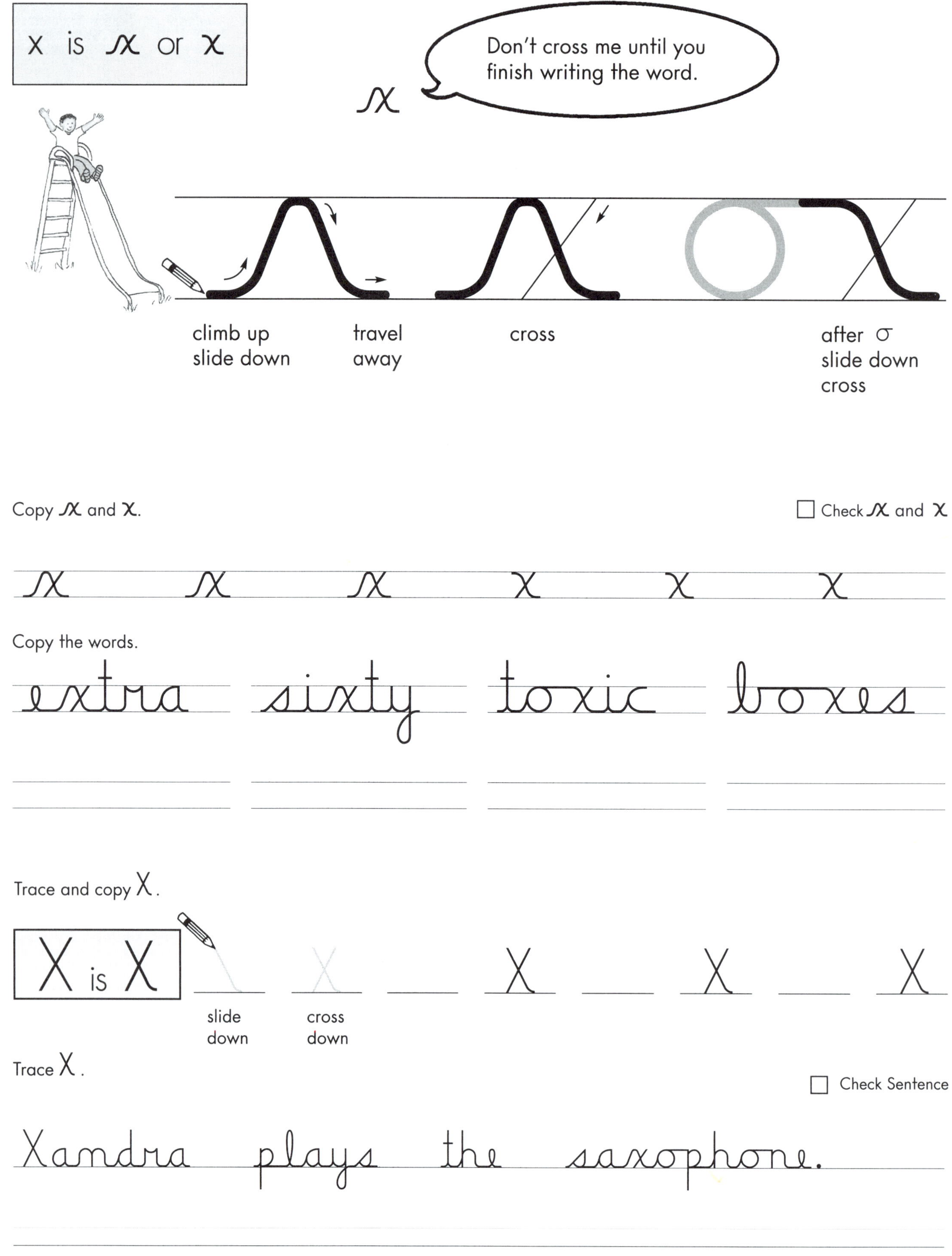

Copy 𝓍 and Χ.

☐ Check 𝓍 and Χ

Copy the words.

extra   sixty   toxic   boxes

Trace and copy Χ.

Trace Χ.

☐ Check Sentence

Xandra plays the saxophone.

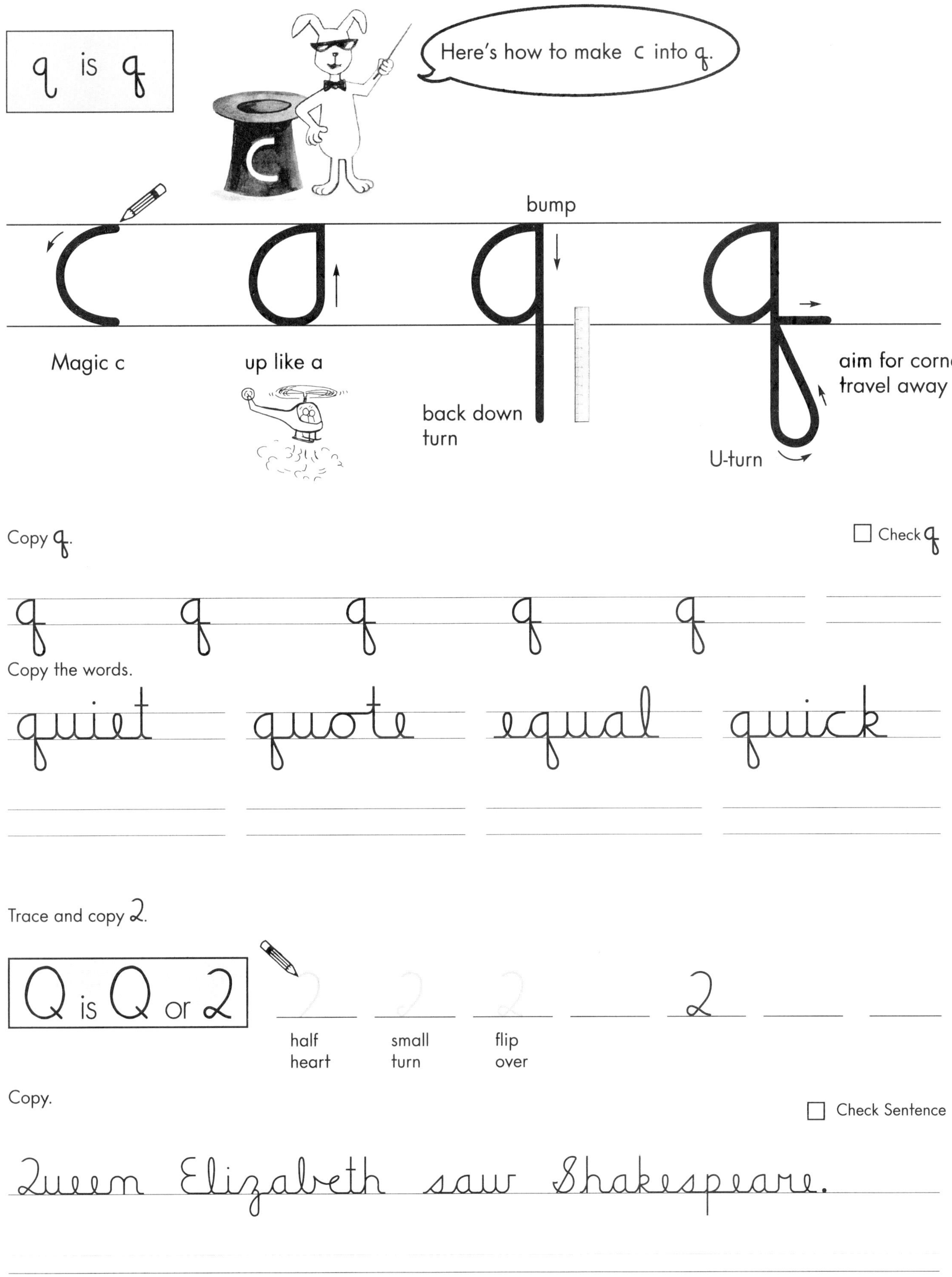

Copy q.

☐ Check q

Copy the words.

quiet   quote   equal   quick

Trace and copy 2.

Q is Q or 2

Copy.

☐ Check Sentence

Queen Elizabeth saw Shakespeare.

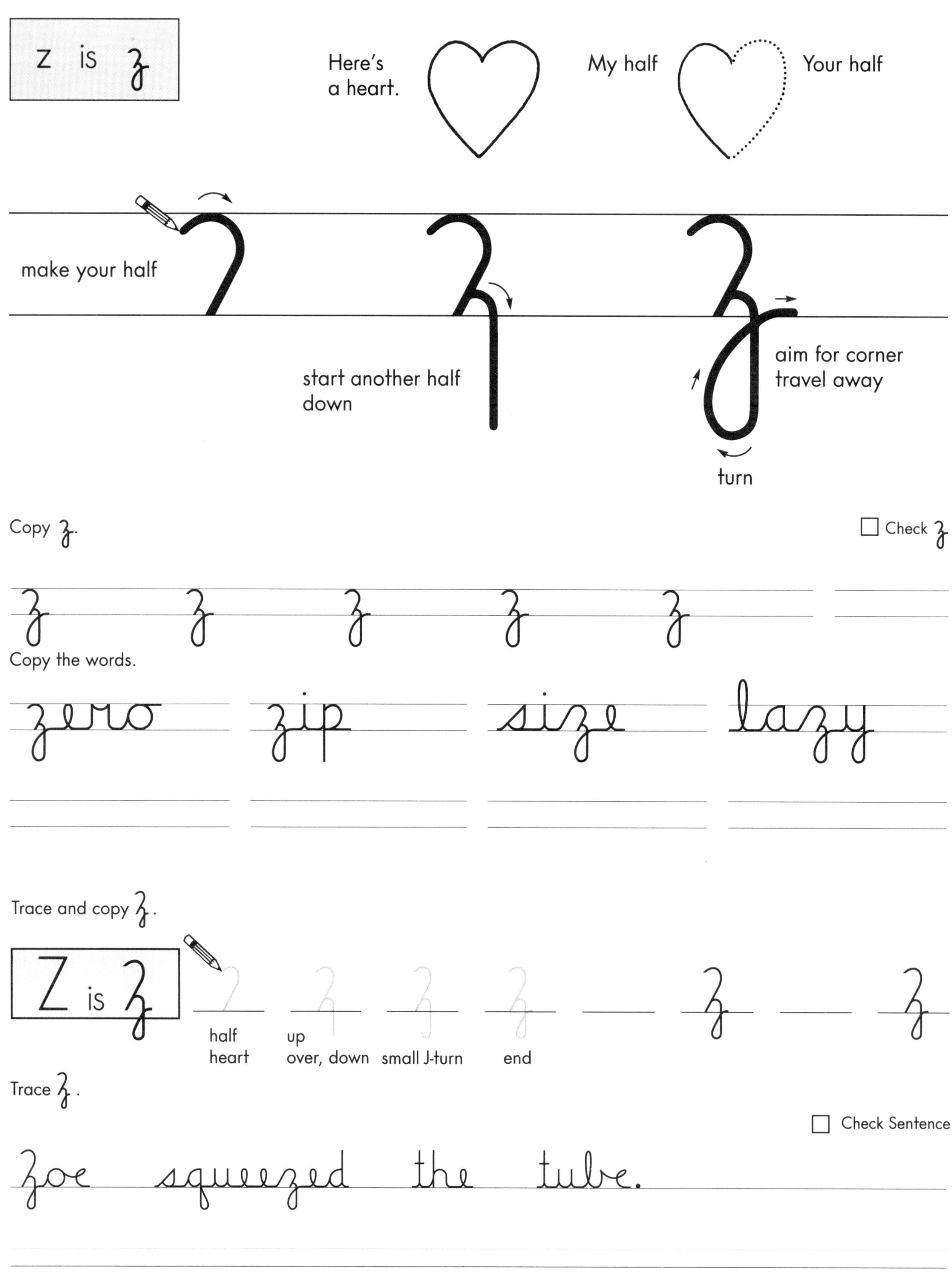

z is z

Here's a heart.
My half
Your half

make your half
start another half down
aim for corner travel away
turn

Copy z.
Check z

Copy the words.
zero   zip   size   lazy

Trace and copy z.
Z is z
half heart   up over, down   small J-turn   end
Trace z.
Check Sentence

Zoe squeezed the tube.

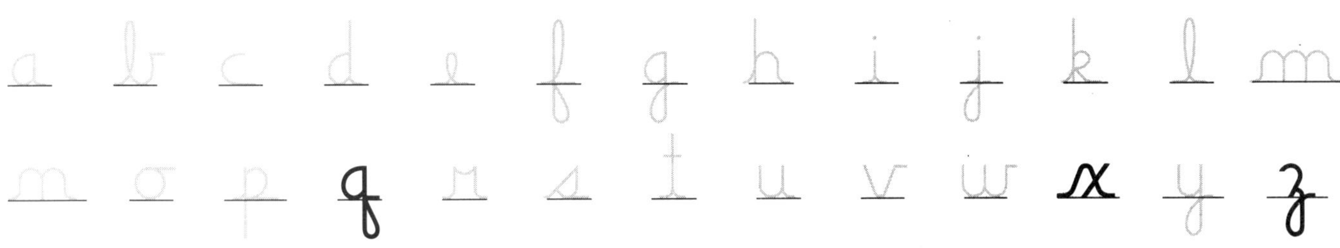

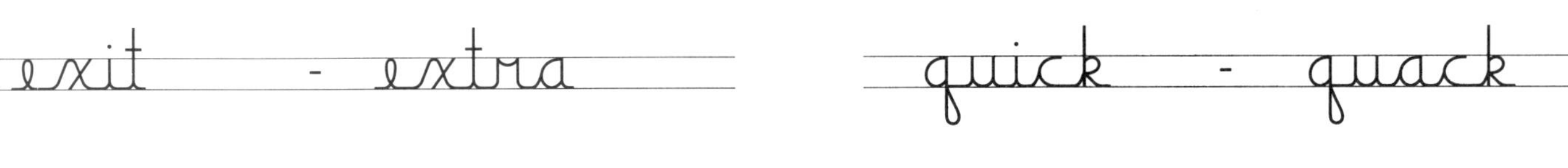

Cursive with new letters: q x z

Wait for the teacher to play the Freeze Game.

exit	- extra	quick	- quack
tax	- fax	maze	- amaze
box	- fox	fizz	- pizza
zoo	- zoom	lax	- relax
aqua	- quail	zen	- zenith

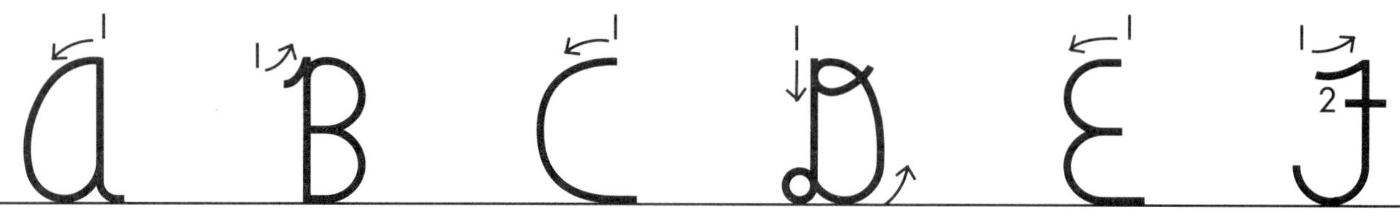

Trace the steps.

Copy the letters, capital cities, and countries.

Magic C   up   back / down

ready down   up around   around again

Magic C

down small turn   flip over   curve up end

c in the air   c again

ready down   J-turn   cross

A Athens, Greece

B Beijing, China

C Canberra, Australia

D Dakar, Senegal

E Edinburgh, Scotland

F Freetown, Sierra Leone

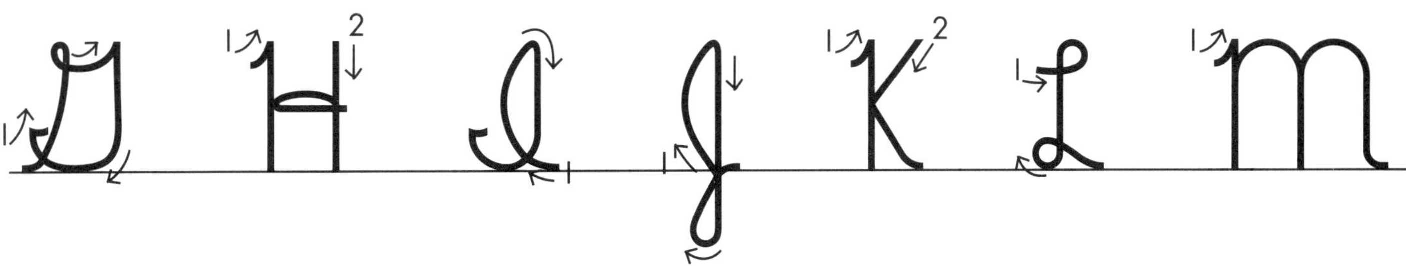

curve up	top like l + i	down big J-turn	end

G Georgetown, Guyana

ready down	down	up over	end

H Havana, Cuba

curve up	down J-turn	end

I Islamabad, Pakistan

curve up	straight down	small J-turn	end

J Jerusalem, Israel

ready down	kick!	slide down

K Kabul, Afghanistan

start with l in the air	down small turn	flip over

L Lima, Peru

ready down	up over down	again

M Moscow, Russia

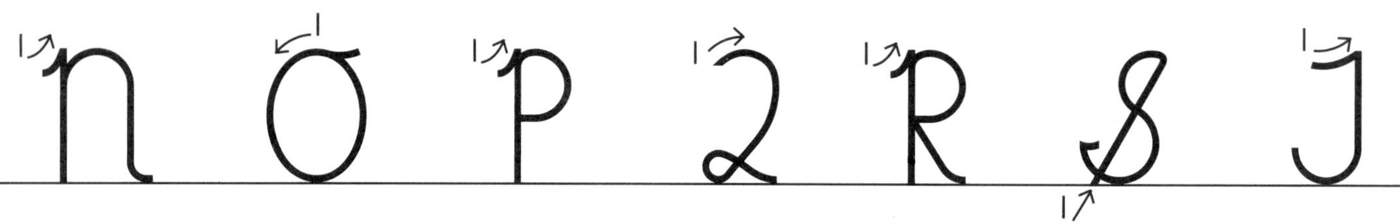

Trace the steps.

ready down	up over down	

Magic C	keep on going	end

ready down	up around

or	half heart	small turn	flip over

ready down	up around	slide down

straight jet takeoff	print S	end

ready down	J-turn

Copy the letters, capitals cities, and the countries.

N Nairobi, Kenya

O Ottawa, Canada

P Paris, France

Q Quito, Ecuador

R Rome, Italy

S Santiago, Chile

J Tokyo, Japan

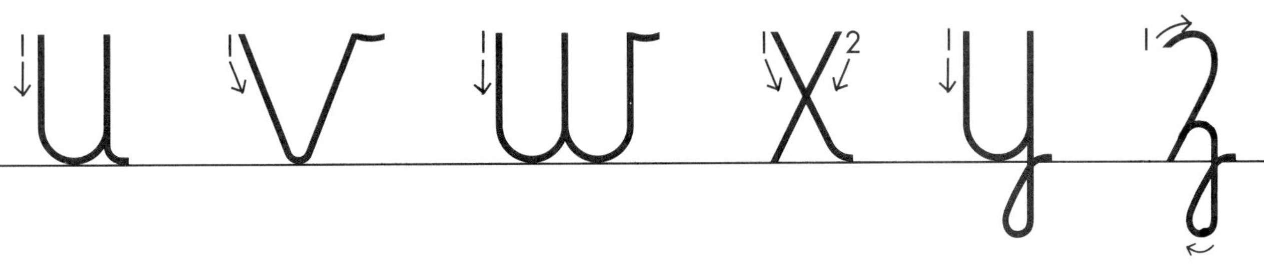

down travel up	back down

U Ulaanbaatar, Mongolia

slide down	up end

V Vienna, Austria

down travel up	again	end

W Warsaw, Poland

slide down	cross down

X X X X X X

down travel up	back down	small J-turn	end

Y Yerevan, Armenia

half heart	up over down	small J-turn	end

Z Zagreb, Croatia

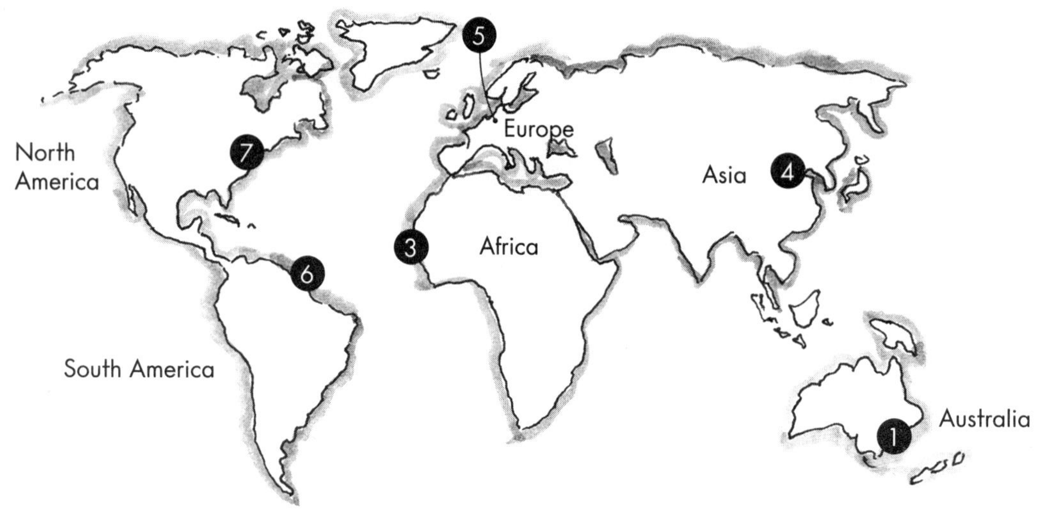

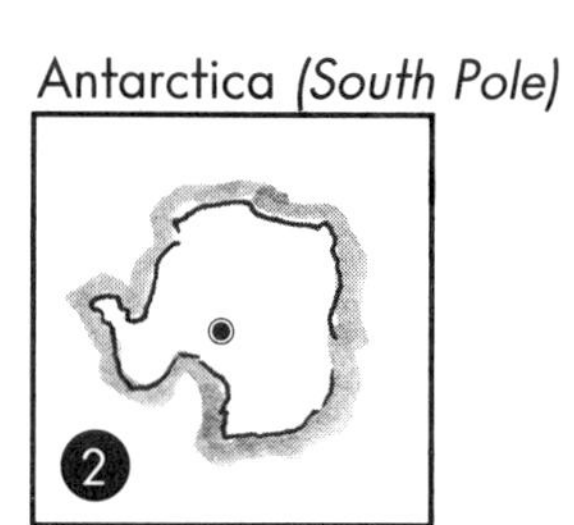

What would you like to do?

1. See white lions in Australia.

2. See Emperor Penguins in Antarctica.

3. Ride a zip line in Dakar, Senegal.

4. Walk on the Great Wall of China.

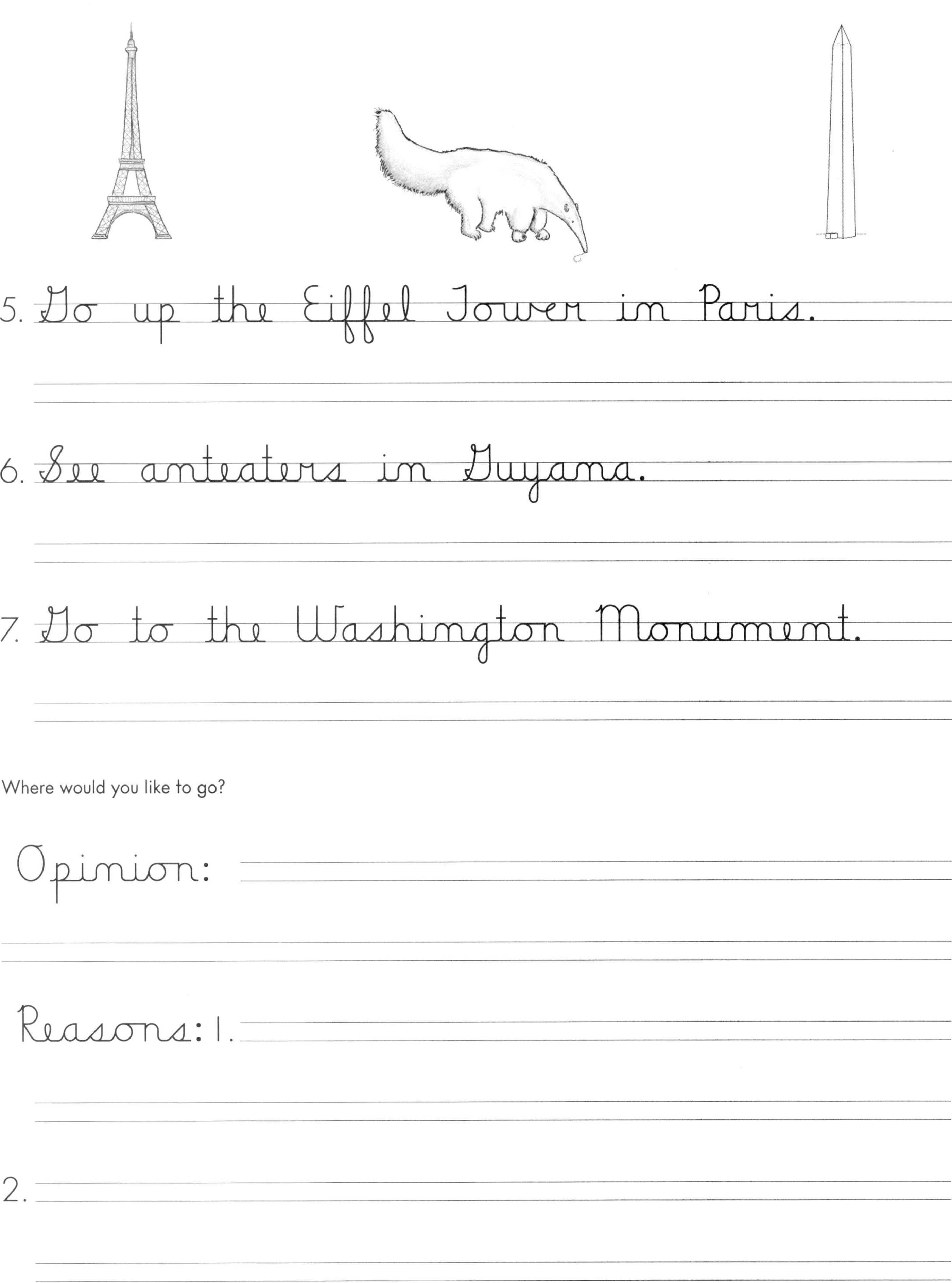

Where would you like to go?

Opinion:

Reasons: 1.

2.

WORDS

Fill in the blanks to make compound words.

 *lady* + *bug* = *ladybug*

 _______ + *shoe* = _______

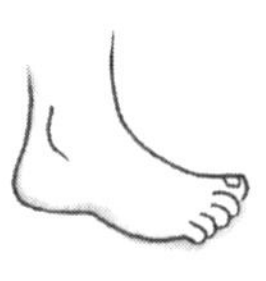 _______ + *ball* = _______

 _______ + *nail* = _______

 _______ + *light* = _______

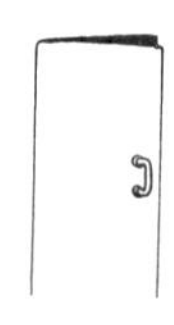 _______ + *knob* = _______

 _______ + *brow* = _______

 _______ + *case* = _______

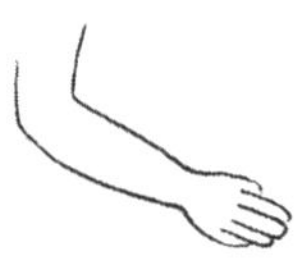 _______ + *chair* = _______

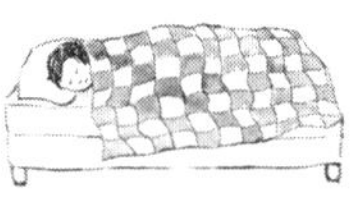 _______ + *room* = _______

WORDS

Some capitals connect and some don't. Connect the capitals that end on the base line and on the right side.
Connect these capitals to the next letter:

$$\mathcal{A} \quad C \quad E \quad \mathcal{G} \quad K \quad L \quad M \quad N \quad \mathcal{R} \quad R \quad U \quad Y \quad Z$$

Your choice:
1. Translate these printed names into cursive.   OR   2. Write different names that start with the same capital.

Ann	________	Noah	________
Christopher	________	Quentin	________
Ella	________	Ryan	________
Jake	________	Uri	________
Katherine	________	Yoko	________
Loren	________	Zachary	________
Matthew	________		

DO NOT connect these capitals to the next letter:

$$B \quad D \quad F \quad G \quad H \quad I \quad O \quad P \quad S \quad J \quad V \quad W \quad X$$

Your choice:
1. Translate these printed names into cursive.   OR   2. Write different names that start with the same capital.

Brad	________	Peter	________
David	________	Samantha	________
Frances	________	Thomas	________
Greg	________	Virginia	________
Hans	________	William	________
Ingrid	________	Xavier	________
Oscar	________		

WORDS

Copy the connections.

o ov ow ol or   w wa wh

b bl bb be br   v ve

Copy the words.

polar bear walrus whale

breathe blow holes blubber

warm blooded born live

PARAGRAPH

Seals bark, whales sing, and polar bears roar. They are social marine mammals. They live in groups and care for their young. Fur or blubber keep them warm, even in the coldest water. These mammals have adapted to marine life.

Copy the paragraph or write your own.

* Capitalize I, the first, last, and important words in book, movie, and song titles.
* Capitalize Ms., Mrs., Miss, Dr., Mr.

CAPITALIZE: Finish the sentences about yourself.

Names   *My name is* _______________________ .

Schools   *My school is* _______________________ .

*Titles, name   *My teacher is* _______________________ .

People   *I admire* _______________________ .

*Movie titles   *I saw* _______________________ .

*Book titles   *I read* _______________________ .

*Song titles   *I can sing* _______________________ .

Restaurant   *My favorite restaurant is* _______________________ .

Cities, towns   *I live in* _______________________ .

Rivers, lakes, oceans   *The closest water is* _______________________ .

Specific places   *I want to visit* _______________________ .

My Opinion

❑ Movie
❑ Book
❑ Performance
❑ Restaurant
Title or Name:
I recommend   because
❑ Movie
❑ Book
❑ Performance
❑ Restaurant
Title or Name:
I recommend   because

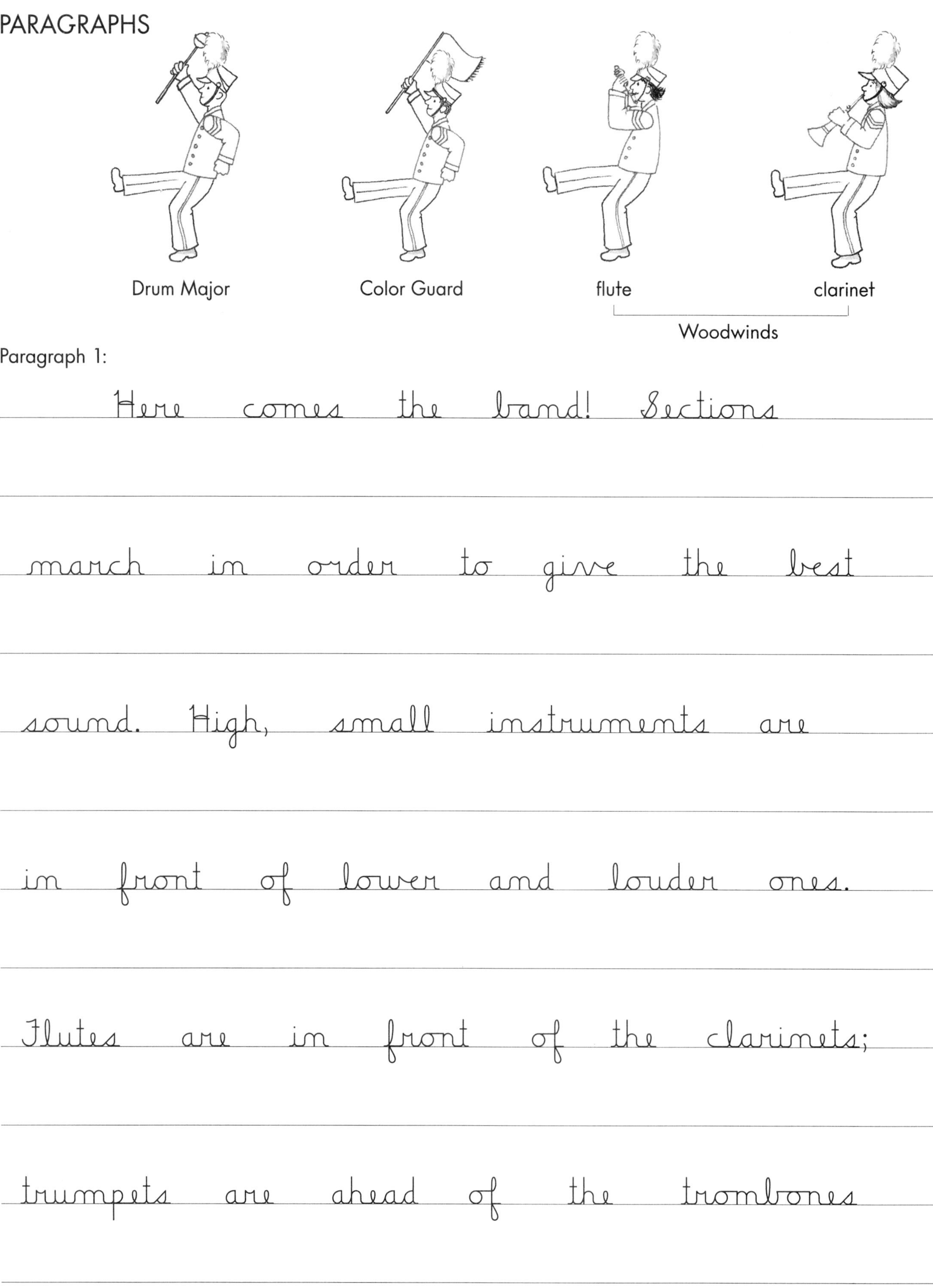

Paragraph 1:

Here comes the band! Sections march in order to give the best sound. High, small instruments are in front of lower and louder ones. Flutes are in front of the clarinets; trumpets are ahead of the trombones

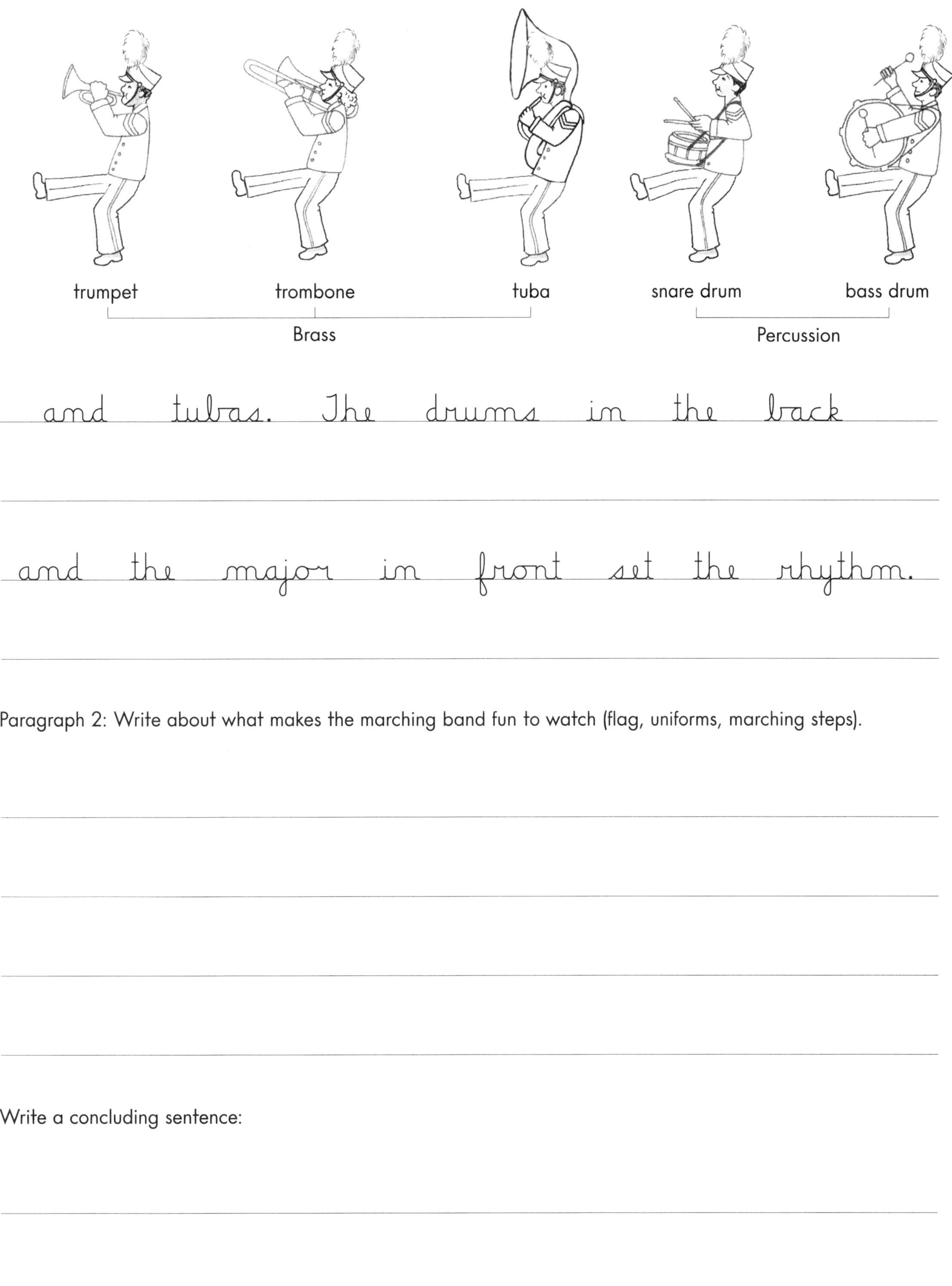

and tubas. The drums in the back

and the major in front set the rhythm.

Paragraph 2: Write about what makes the marching band fun to watch (flag, uniforms, marching steps).

Write a concluding sentence:

GREEK GLOSSARY

Copy the bold, Greek words in cursive.

auto = self **bio** = life **geo** = earth **graph** = write, draw **micro** = small

_______ _______ _______ _______ _______

phon = sound **photo** = light **poly** = many **scope** = look at **tele** = for

_______ _______ _______ _______ _______

Φ

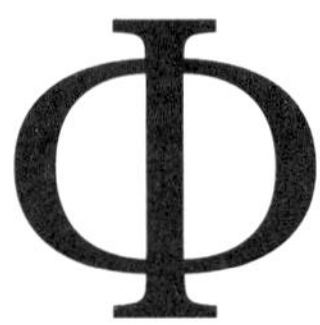

This is the Greek Letter Phi.
Phi is pronounced fi. Many English
words are based on Greek words.
In these words, ph sounds like /f/.

Find and underline the **ph** in these English words.

apostro<u>ph</u>e, triumph, trophy,

philosopher, autograph, biography,

geography, photograph, dolphin,

microphone, physics, Sophia

Write the definitions of four words with "ph." Choose from the listed words.

○	

Copy the names.

Galileo
- February 15, 1564
- Born Pisa, Italy
- Physicist, astronomer
- Improved telescope
- Saw Jupiter's moons
- Earth revolves around sun
- Laws of speed/falling things

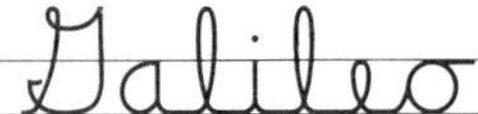

Isaac Newton
- January 4, 1643
- Born Woolsthrope, England
- Mathematician, astronomer
- Laws of motion and gravity
- Gravity makes things fall
- Planets revolve around sun

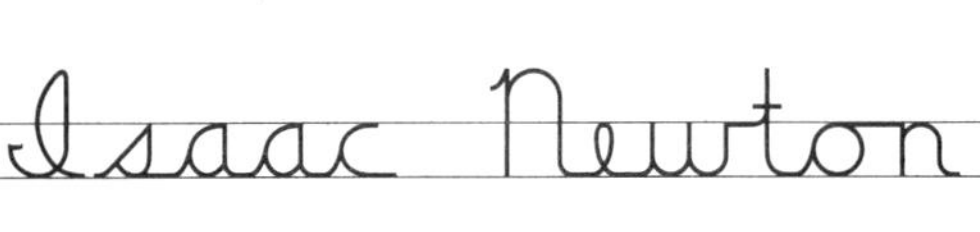

Marie Curie
- November 7, 1867
- Born Warsaw, Poland
- Moved to Paris
- Professor of Physics
- Nobel Prize winner
- Discovered radium

Marie Curie

Vera Rubin
- July 23, 1928
- Born Philadelphia, PA
- Astrophysicist
- As teen built a telescope
- Studied motion of stars
- Galaxy rotation
- Confirmed dark matter invisible, 90% of universe

Vera Rubin

Write about one of these scientists.

Mnemonics are memory aids. You can remember a sentence to remember the planets. In 2006, astronomers decided that Pluto was not a planet. So, now there are only eight planets.

Copy.

Mercury   Venus   Earth   Mars

My   Very   Excited   Mother

Make up a mnemonic sentence.

M   V   E   M

ACRONYMS

Acronyms are words made from the initial letters of other words.

Copy.

SCUBA is an acronym for:

S Self   C Contained   U Underwater

Jupiter   Saturn   Uranus   Neptune

Jumped   Straight   Up   North.

J   S   U   N

B Breathing   A Apparatus

Eugenie Clark, the "Shark Lady"
- Born May 4, 1922
- Ic-thy-ol-o-gist
- Greek: icthy = fish
- Ologist = one who studies

She was a swimmer and a girl who loved sharks. People thought sharks were dumb killers. She didn't. She spent years studying them.

With SCUBA gear and shark  repellent, she swam with sharks and did important research.

The Flounder

The flounder is a funny fish,
Sort of flat, like a dish,
One side up, the other down,
Eyes on top to look around.

Copy the poem.

FYI means: for your information. Here is information
for you about flounders:

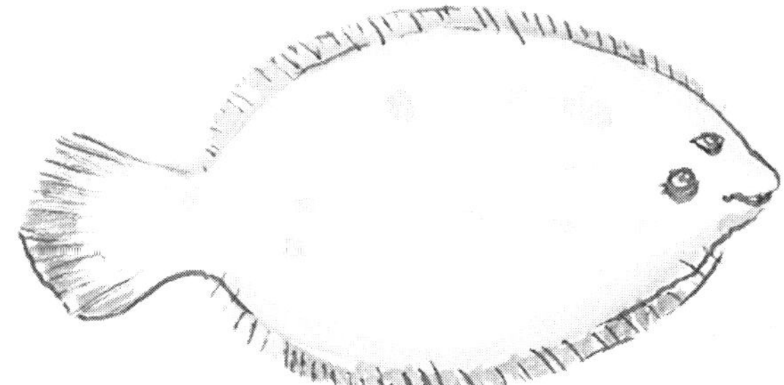

Flounder Facts:

- Flatfish
- Five different species
- Size depends on species 5–25"
- Found on sandy ocean floors
- Feeds on small fish, shrimp, or crabs
- Bottom is white
- Top is mottled for camouflage

Synonyms are words that share the same, or almost the same, meaning.
Synonym starts with s, just like same and similar.

GREEK	**syn**	same
	onym	name or word

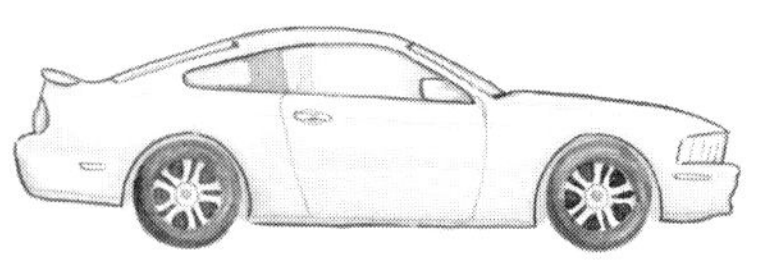

automobile

car

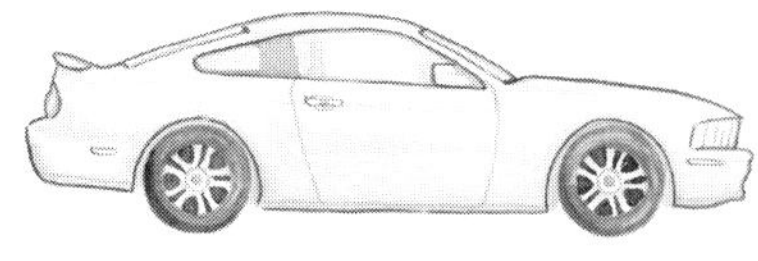

vehicle

Translate each printed word into cursive.
Write a synonym beside it.

automobile   *automobile*   =   *car*

boat   _________________   =

cheerful   _________________   =

elderly   _________________   =

intelligent   _________________   =

purchase   _________________   =

street   _________________   =

student   _________________   =

woman   _________________   =

Antonyms are words that mean the opposite.

GREEK	**ant** against
	onym name or word

short

long

Translate each printed word into cursive.
Write an antonym beside it.

difficult   *difficult*   ≠   *easy*

expensive ____________________ ≠ ______________

chilly ____________________ ≠ ______________

generous ____________________ ≠ ______________

interesting ____________________ ≠ ______________

Write two sentences with antonyms. Example: My grandfather is **old**, but I am **young**.

1. ____

____

2. ____

____

Galileo
February 15, 1564–January 8, 1642

Go to Italy! See the Leaning Tower of Pisa. People say that's where Galileo dropped two cannon balls, one heavy, one light, to see which one would land first.

For centuries people believed Aristotle, the Greek philosopher who claimed that the heavier one would land first. Galileo proved him wrong. They landed together. That's physics!

Copy the paragraph.

WORDS

Copy.

PREFIXES

equi-, sym- = same

A + 7 = 14

equation

quad- = 4

quadrilateral

kilo- = 1,000

5 Kilometers = 3.10 Miles

kilometer

dia- = through

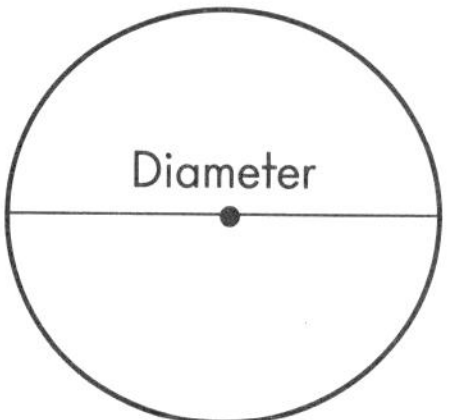

diameter

rect- = right

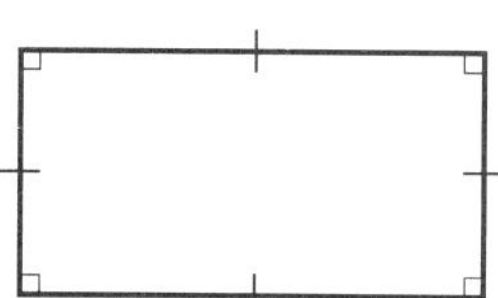

rectangle

WORD ROOTS

later = side

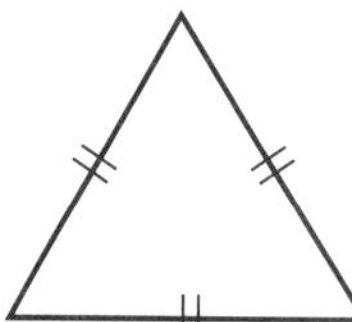

equilateral

meter = measure

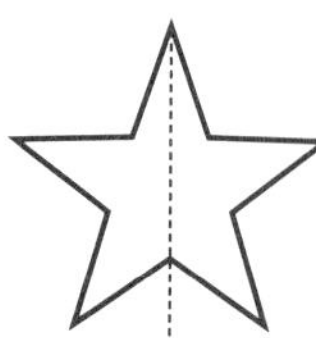

symmetry

PARAGRAPH

We measure dimensions. String
has one dimension: length. Flat
shapes have two: length and width.
Solid shapes have three dimensions:
length, width, and height.

List two-dimensional and three-dimensional shapes.

Rectangle   Oval   Square   Circle   Triangle   Cube   Cylinder   Triangular prism   Cone   Pyramid

1. ___________________   1. ___________________

2. ___________________   2. ___________________

3. ___________________   3. ___________________

4. ___________________   4. ___________________

5. ___________________   5. ___________________

PARAGRAPHS

People first began measuring with their
bodies. They measured thickness with thumbs,
horses with hands, boards with feet, and cloth
with an arm. These measurements became standardized.

Copy the paragraph. Indent the first word.

Fill in the blanks with the missing unit of measurement.

4 inches = 1 _hand_

12 inches = 1 _____________

36 inches = 3 _____________ = 1 _____________

5,280 feet = 1 _____________

The metric system of measurement

developed as math and science

advanced. The basic unit is the meter.

Smaller and larger units are in

decimals or multiples of ten.

This is part of a meter. It is 1 decimeter long.
10 centimeters
100 millimeters

dm

cm 1   2   3   4   5   6   7   8   9   10
mm 10 20 30 40 50 60 70 80 90 100

Copy words in cursive.

mm   cm   dm   m
millimeter   <   centimeter   <   decimeter   <   meter

<   <   <

WORDS

Homonyms are words that have the same sound and the same spelling. Homonyms have different meanings. Dictionaries list and number the different meanings.

wave   wave

Write a sentence for each homonym.
Example: Sam's mom said, "**Wave** good-bye."
       He saw a **wave** in the ocean.

bat -

bat -

bug -

bug -

hide -

hide -

seal -

seal -

ring -

ring -

Homophones are words that have the same sound, but have different meanings and spellings.

see   sea

Homophones

Eye and I, see and sea,
Won and one, ate and eight,
So and sew, knew and new
Homophones are fun to do.

Copy the poem in cursive.

WORDS

Directions:

1. Look up each word.

2. On the first line, write the part of speech.
   The dictionary uses abbreviations for the parts
   of speech. Here is the key:

   n.   = noun
   adj. = adjective
   v.   = verb
   adv. = adverb

3. On the second line, write the definition.

beet

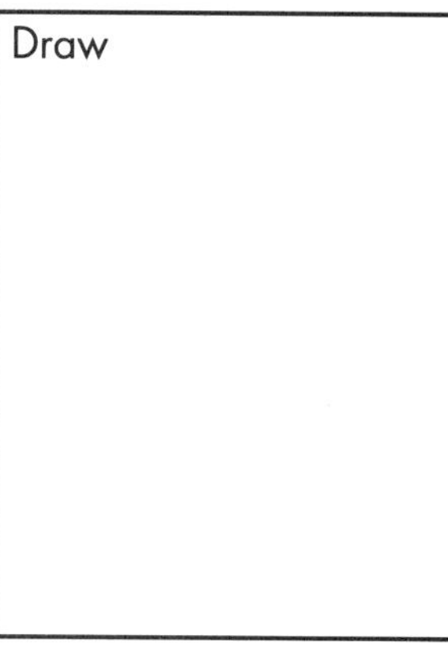

beetle

amp = noun

a unit of electricity

ample =

beet =

beetle =

sing =

single =

Libraries organize their books.

Biographies are shelved alphabetically by the subject's name. Fiction is shelved by the author's name. Nonfiction uses a set of numbers, the Dewey Decimal system.

Wait for the teacher. Fill in the categories.

000 General Knowledge	500
100	600
200	700
300	800
400	900 Geography, History

PHRASES

Similes compare two things that are not really alike, but share a common feature.
Similes use the words **like** or **as**.

- **as** a rock
- **like** a dream
- **like** a monkey
- **as** a feather
- **like** a fish
- **as** molasses

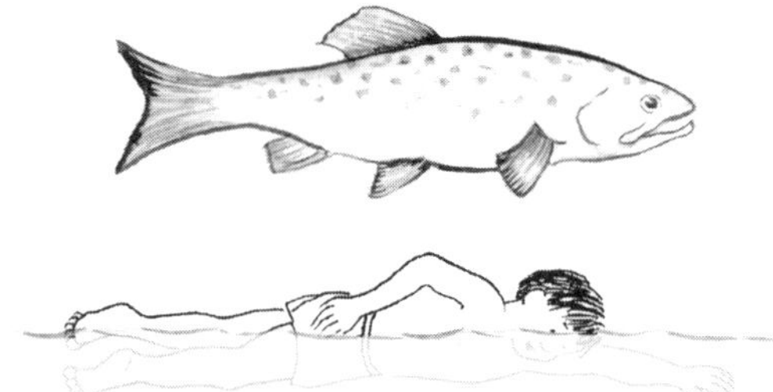

Complete each sentence with a simile from the above list.

Charlie swims ____________________.

This bed is as hard ____________________.

He climbs ____________________.

I can lift it. It's as light ____________________.

Hurry up! You're as slow ____________________.

This car drives ____________________.

METAPHORS

Metaphors are figures of speech. Metaphors actually say one thing is something else in order to describe it better.

Copy.

That car is a lemon!

That test was a piece of cake.

Take Out!

I could write do not, but I don't
I could write will not, but I won't
I like contractions, they're fun to do,
Take out a letter, or take out a few.

Copy the poem in cursive.

A **contraction** is a short form of a word. An **apostrophe** ' takes place of an omitted letter or letters.

Write out the long form of these contractions in cursive.

we're	you're	doesn't	don't
they're	she's	it's	won't

a B C D E F G H I J K L M
N O P 2 R S Ⓙ U V W X Y Z

Choose your six favorite letters. Circle them.
Now write a fun sentence to feature each letter.

J   Jamiko tasted teriyaki in Tokyo.

FRIENDLY LETTER

Write a thank you letter. Organize your letter like this.

Date
Month Day, Year

Greeting
Dear _________________ ,

Body
Say, "thank you" and tell how much you appreciate the gift or help. Mention what it is or what they did. Add details to make it more personal.

Use a comma:
1. After the day of the month
2. After the greeting
3. After the closing

Closing
Sincerely, Thank you, or Love,

Signature

PARAGRAPHS

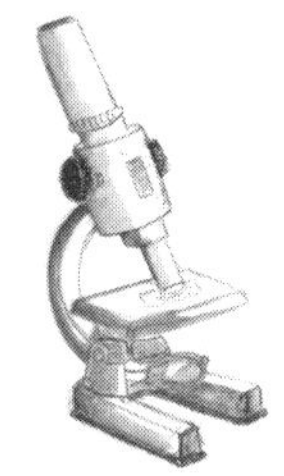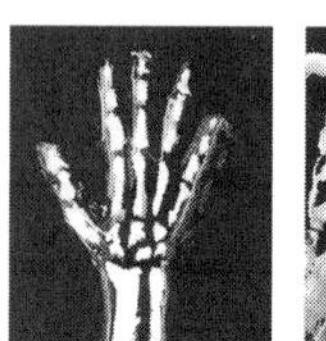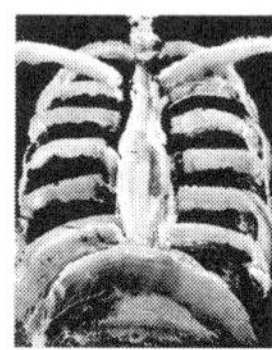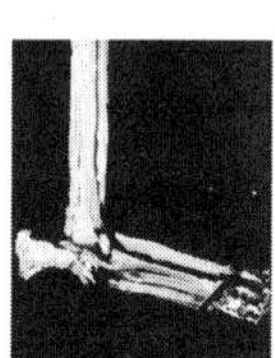

Write a draft.

1. Tell your reader what you're going to say. That's your topic.

Two inventions changed medicine.

Or

Two inventions save lives.

2. Say it. List ideas or information about your topic. Don't use complete sentences, just get down your ideas.

Microscope

- see invisible things

- see germs

- see cells

X-ray

- see inside bodies

- see bones

- see metal

3. Finish by telling your reader what you said in different words.

Two inventions help doctors.

Or

Microscopes and X-rays save lives.

Use the draft on page 88 to write one or two paragraphs. Remember to indent each paragraph.

PARAGRAPHS

Write a draft.

1. Tell your reader what you're going to say. That's your topic.

My topic:

2. Say it. List ideas or information about your topic. Don't use complete sentences, just get down your ideas.

About my topic:

-
-
-
-
-
-

3. Finish by telling your reader what you said in different words.

My topic restated:

Write one or two paragraphs. Remember to indent the first sentence.

SENTENCES

Quotations are a person's exact words.

William Shakespeare
1564–1616

Copy the famous quotes like this:

William Shakespeare said, "All the world's a stage."

Frederick Douglass
1818–1895

Louis Armstrong
1901–1971

Anne Frank
1929–1945

Neil Armstrong
1930–2012

WHAT DID THEY MEAN?

Remember, we learned that a metaphor is a figure of speech. There are three metaphors in these quotations. Discuss them in your class.

"All the world's a stage."   How can the world be a stage?

"What we play is life."   How could a trumpet play life?

"That's...one giant leap for mankind."   How could mankind take a leap?

     Cursive Success   **93**

Graduation

by Sherry Landes

I used to think cursive was confusing,

I look back now and that's amusing,

I learned it's easy to connect each letter,

Now, I write faster and my work looks better.